ILLUSTRATED
MARTIAL ARTS & SPORTS IN JAPAN
[日本の武道]

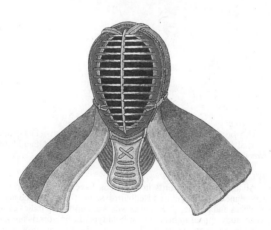

ILLUSTRATED
MARTIAL ARTS & SPORTS IN JAPAN

1st edition........1993

Printed in Japan

About this Book

1) Layout
    This book consists of the following seven sections (1) Japanese Martial Arts (2) Sumō (3) Jūdō (4) Kendō (5) Karaté (6) Other Martial Arts (7) Modern-day Sports in Japan

2) Japanese Words
    All the Japanese words in this book have been romanized in accordance with the revised Hepburn system. Except for the names of places and people, all Japanese words are printed in italics except where they appear in headings or bold type. Long vowels are indicated by a line above, as in *'Shintō'*; and, since e's are pronounced "ay" in Japanese, e's at the ends of words are marked with an acute accent, as in *'saké'* (pronounced "sakay").

Dear Readers

●

Everyone visiting Japan wants to know what makes the country tick. And most hope, in some way, to take an active part in the vibrant society of today's Japan. The world of sports allows you to do this, all the while having a good time.

By learning a little about Japan's traditional martial arts, handed down from generation to generation, you will better understand the spirit of Japan, and catch a glimpse of Japan's changing history. Aristocratic ceremonies of the distant past gave us sumō. Later, military government and civil strife led to a martial spirit and refined military techniques, with ninja spies and subterfuge lurking in the background. Defeat in war brought a further refinement, with the goal being purely self-defense.

And the present: Japanese are working fewer hours and enjoying a more sporting life, as spectators or as participants. Join in the fun too! The more you know about a sport, the more you will enjoy it.

CONTENTS

Chapter 3 JŪDŌ
第3章 柔道

Chapter 4 KENDŌ
第4章　剣道

Chapter 5 KARATÉ
第5章　空手

Chapter 6 OTHER MARTIAL ARTS
第6章　その他の武道

Chapter 7 MODERN-DAY SPORTS IN JAPAN
第7章　日本でさかんなスポーツ

COLUMN

JAPANESE MARTIAL ARTS

日本の武道

Centuries of dedication have been spent in the practice of Japanese martial arts. As examples of martial arts, or *budō,* we could give jūdō, kendō, karaté, kyūdō (archery), and naginata (halberd wielding), and to this same group we could add sumō wrestling. All martial arts practiced today have come down to us from ancient *bujutsu* (military techniques).

Looked at through the ages we see that the word *'budō'* contains many ideas. Today *budō* is represented in a number of combat-type sports. But the term once referred to a military way of living, and the way a soldier should perform his skills (whether in archery, horseback riding, swordsmanship, the javelin or whatever). *'Budō'* also relates to *bushidō,* the ethical and philosophical life of a *samurai.*

Looking back at the origins of *bujutsu,* or *budō* techniques, we see many variations. In ancient times a *samurai* could protect himself and could knock over opponents in a number of ways, with weapons or without. If weapons were used, which ones, and how? Many choices were open. And so it is that the world of *bujutsu* separated into a number of different martial arts.

Before *samurai* gained prominence in Japan the aristocracy was at the apex of society. About the only combat promoted at that time was sumō wrestlers grappling practically naked in ceremonies for the Imperial Court and its entourage of aristocrats. But in the Kamakura period (1192-1333) and thereafter military governments and their *samurai* enjoyed prominence. Warriors gained experience on the battlefield and developed a number of military skills known as *bujutsu*. These included the secrets of the bow and arrow, the sword, the javelin, and horseback riding.

In the 16th century law and order broke down and a period of civil strife ensued. From this time until the Edo era (1603-1867) *bujutsu* techniques and teachings were gradually systematized into a number of different schools, or styles. Schools only developed after the appearance of an exceptional master who gathered around him many disciples. Before a specific skill could become part of a school of its own other conditions had to be met; these included many long hours of guidance and training, and the formation of an organization that could pass this specialized knowledge down to others.

With the advent of different styles of martial art, *bujutsu* became more than just a practical way to knock over an opponent. It developed into a way of life that found meaning in mastering martial techniques. To overthrow an enemy any weapon or a combination of weapons will do: but the various styles of martial art all emphasized the mastery of one specific area of concentration, for example the sword or the javelin. Thus, as previously mentioned, *bujutsu* separated into a variety of disciplines.

Experts in the early Edo period (first part of the 17th century) studied *bujutsu* theory and set it down on paper. These studies are still extant in the form of books and *makimono* scrolls. Because the Edo era experienced a long period of peace, *bushi* (warriors) had no real role to perform, so their study of *bujutsu* became more and more theoretical. Each school vied with the others, searching for an art ever more refined. Emphasis was placed on training, on acquiring the culture and prerequisite accomplishments of the warrior class.

As *bujutsu* became more theoretical it developed ties with different philosophical systems such as Zen, Confucianism and Taoism. This spiritual side of *bujutsu* took on much importance: practice of techniques and development of the body and reflexes were no longer enough.

By the middle of the Edo period the *bushi* spirit had become dulled by continual peace. *Bujutsu,* stripped of its practical, pugnacious side, focused only on theory and formalism. This naturally left it open to criticism.

However, at the end of the Edo era Japanese society was again subjected to stress. Foreign ships off-shore were regarded as a threat; opinions became seriously divided on a number of issues. This gave new importance to *bujutsu,* so that not only the military class but also the ordinary citizen looked to it for support.

The age of the *samurai* died with the advent of the Meiji period in 1868, and *bujutsu* influences waned with the new push towards modernization and westernization. *Bujutsu* was no longer taught in schools, as the authorities considered such purely Japanese ways out of keeping with the age.

But war followed: first the Sino-Japanese War of 1894-95, then the Russo-Japanese War in 1904-05, then World War I. With the accompanying rise of nationalism, *bujutsu* was again introduced into the school curriculum. Kendō and jūdō were two martial arts to gain prominence at this time. In about 1931 kendō and jūdō became required subjects at junior high schools and men's normal schools. The purpose here was to develop a national mentality, one based on physical strength, courage and a no-nonsense spirit.

This use of martial arts for military purposes, with its emphasis on patriotism and militarism, led to the banning of this kind of education after the nation's defeat in World War II. In time, though, such skills as jūdō, kendō and sumō gained recognition as sports, and again earned their place in school instruction.

It was during the 1964 Olympic Games, held in Tokyo, that jūdō was added as an official Olympic sport. This is one reason why Japanese martial arts gained interest world-wide. In addition, a Hawaiian earned the highest title in sumō, *yokozuna* in 1993. Yet even in the midst of all this internationalization the essential spirit of budō martial art, handed down in an unbroken line from the distant past, continues to influence Japanese society today.

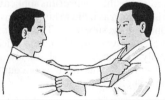

The *samurai* warrior of old was expected to exhibit certain moral characteristics, especially those extolled by Confucius. All followers of martial arts were to strive after the following ethical attributes:

Jin (Benevolence) 仁

Forgiveness and kindness have been praised over the centuries. *Jin* is these, the highest of all human attributes; it is love, charity. For the *samurai* benevolence meant defending the ideals of justice and morality which the austere military society in those days held. The world was viewed with an unflappable aura of empathy, though sympathy did not show its weak side.

Chi (Wisdom) 智

A true interpretation of the writings of ancient sages points out to us the absolute necessity of distinguishing between good and evil, between right and wrong. This is *chi,* or true wisdom. The *samurai* was taught that wisdom lay in complete control over one's own volitions. *Chi* is the knowledge of many things, but it is more: it is to have the courage to put into practice the ideals sages since ancient times have given us.

Rei (Propriety) 礼

Rei, or propriety, is respect towards others. By maintaining an exterior appearance of esteem for others, and by abiding by polite formalities, the inner soul too will come to feel the same respect that is shown outwardly. For the *samurai* this applied to his relations with ordinary mortals as much as it did to his relationship with his Shinto gods, the Buddha, and his superiors. This feeling of reverence is to be projected just the correct amount, not too much, not too little, and always impartially. Japanese martial arts are noted for bows and respectful demeanor; this exterior show of courtesy leads to a heart with similar inclinations.

勇 *Yū* (Courage)

The *samurai* was expected to show no fear whenever he realized what was the just thing to do. True courage (*yū*), it was said, was to live when living was important, and to die when dying was the proper thing to do. In times of peace courage was still required, though it might take different forms: perpetual loyalty to one's lord, ready to fight for him if fighting became necessary; diligence in the arts of the pen and the sword; a frugal and simple life; and, a stoicism prepared for anything.

義 *Gi* (Righteousness)

Bushi ideals were rigorous, and the most rigorous of all was the command to defend what is right and proper. Righteousness (*gi*) means the ability to know what is right, to follow that road without hesitation, to die when dying is the right thing to do, to kill when killing is the proper course of action.

誠 *Makoto* (Sincerity)

Makoto means treating people kindly, without falsehood of any kind. It means knowing what is right, deceiving neither those around us nor ourselves, showing love, sincerity and respect toward all. The *samurai* was prepared to prove his sincerity by cutting his finger and using the bloody fingerprint as a seal under his signature. It was said that those who showed sincerity would never fail in the long run.

名誉 *Meiyo* (Honor)

Honor was held in the highest esteem. *Meiyo,* honor, was achieved through glorious deeds which earned for the *samurai* his rank above the merchant and agricultural peasant classes. The *samurai* was never to sully the name of his ancestors; he was to strive always for a higher position, thereby increasing the honor of his clan.

The Japanese have developed a number of sayings which express their admiration for the attributes described on the previous two pages. The following maxims will help you gain an understanding of Japanese martial arts and the inner workings of the Japanese mind.

Shintō o mekkyaku sureba hi mo mata suzushi
<Even flames are cool for those who clear their minds of unnecessary thoughts.>

By achieving a frame of mind completely uncluttered of irrelevant thoughts you will be able to transcend any difficulty and fear nothing. This ideal was demanded of the *samurai,* who had to be ready for death at any time. In Japan this saying is commonly used even for those training in today's *dōjō.*

Manabité omowazareba sunawachi kurashi
<Books in themselves are of little value without reason.>

This saying is found in the Analects of Confucius. It tells us that all the book learning in the world is of little value if you do not meditate and cogitate on what you read. Applied to martial arts, this aphorism tells us there is no point in superficial training; practice is only made perfect by continually grasping the whole scheme of things, both theoretical and practical. Only by such day to day diligence can you become truly learned and respectable.

Michi ni oité wa shi o itowazu
<An expert fears not even death itself.>

This saying is attributed to the famous swordsman, Musashi Miyamoto. In the 17th century, when he lived, to become truly proficient in martial arts one had to be prepared for anything, even death. Such strength of mind is still needed by those who practice a martial art today.

Zengo saidan
<Rid yourself of the past and the future.>

This Buddhist aphorism, adopted by martial artists, warns against being attached to things which are long gone, and against worrying about the future. Instead, we must concentrate on things which are at hand at the moment. This is an important principle to be followed in martial art training.

Mizukara hikuu sureba tattoshi
<Respect comes to those who are meek.>

This saying, originating in ancient Chinese literature, indicates that to earn respect you must act humbly. You should regard your opponent with humility when practicing a martial art.

Chi-ni ité ran o wasurezu
<Remain ready for war even in times of peace.>

Even in peacetime remain on guard, because conflict could easily break out again. A *samurai* must be prepared to set out for battle at a moment's notice. Applied to martial arts, an expert must be ready at all times to defend or counterattack.

In ancient China and Japan all martial arts were classified into eighteen different branches, the *Bugei Jū-Happan*. Eighteen is only a rough estimation: Chinese and Japanese disciplines differed from each other, and the passage of time brought about other changes too. But if we wish to make an incomplete list of martial arts which have come down to us from ancient times we could come up with the following. (Words in brackets indicate the area of skill.) *Bajutsu* (horsemanship), *kyūjutsu* (archery), *kenjutsu* (swordsmanship), *sōjutsu* (the javelin), *battōjutsu* (drawing a sword), *suijutsu* (swimming), *jittejutsu* (the truncheon), *tantōjutsu* (the dagger), *shurikenjutsu* (knife throwing), *ganshinjutsu* (the needle), *naginatajutsu* (the halberd), *hōjutsu* (artillery), *toritejutsu* (restraining), *jūjutsu* (self-defense without weapons), *bōjutsu* (the stave), *kusarigamajutsu* (the sickle and chain), *mojirijutsu* (the hook), and *shinobijutsu* (*ninja* stealth).

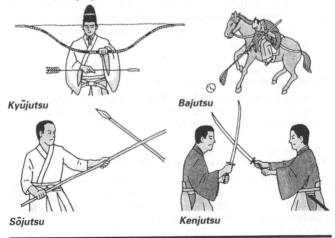

Kyūjutsu

Bajutsu

Sōjutsu

Kenjutsu

Shurikenjutsu

Naginatajutsu

Bōjutsu

Kusarigamajutsu

Martial Arts and the Japanese

Japanese martial arts put great emphasis on courtesy. When sportsmen and women first meet each other before a bout, they stand with back straight (or sit respectfully in the *seiza* position, explained on page 82) and gaze directly into the other's eyes, then bow. Every sport stresses respect for one's opponent. Such respect is also important in the daily lives of Japanese people, especially when meeting someone for the first time or greeting superiors. All businessmen must keep this point in mind.

In martial arts dedication is as important as courtesy. One is expected to avoid all sensual pleasure and desire, striving instead for spiritual and physical excellence. This same dedication is seen in other sports in Japan as well, not only martial arts.

Martial arts as practiced today are far removed from the idea of doing battle with an enemy. Rather, each participant aims at becoming an all-round man or woman with a sound mind in a sound body.

SUMŌ
相撲

SUMŌ THROUGH THE AGES

相撲の歴史

One of Japan's uniquenesses can be seen in sumō, an ancient form of wrestling. Two men, wearing only a loincloth, have only their bare hands to compete in a raised ring, the object being to push the other man out of the ring, or to knock him over. The clothes worn, the mannerisms, and the polite formalities all show us vividly some of Japan's ancient customs; this helps explain why this national sport of Japan is so popular.

The Uniqueness of Sumō

The two wrestlers, practically naked, try to win over the other. Being large and heavy is a distinct advantage, but a smaller wrestler's technique can enable him to knock his opponent over.

The bout starts with polite formalities, and ends the same way. Like jūdō, kendō and other martial arts, it is important that sumō wrestlers show respect for their opponents.

The wrestlers are often immense, but they need agility and quick reflexes. It is relatively easy to judge the winner, and victory comes quickly: you need only force your opponent to touch the ground with a part of his body other than the soles of his feet, or push him outside the ring.

Ancient Sumō

Sumō's roots go back many centuries. In ancient times sumō was a Shintō rite: the outcome of ritual matches (*shinji-zumō*) was used to predict agricultural yield. Later the Emperor promoted sumō as a form of entertainment. Burly wrestlers were invited from all over Japan to compete once a year in his presence at meets called *tenran-zumō*.

In those days there was no ring or referee.

Only the Emperor, aristocrats and important government officials could attend. Lesser court officials were not even allowed to take a peak.

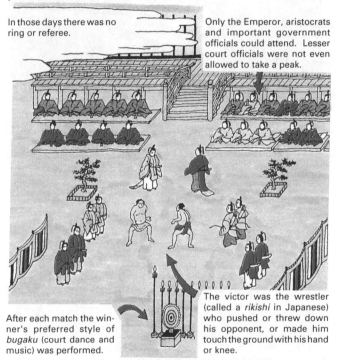

After each match the winner's preferred style of *bugaku* (court dance and music) was performed.

The victor was the wrestler (called a *rikishi* in Japanese) who pushed or threw down his opponent, or made him touch the ground with his hand or knee.

In the aristocratic society of the Heian period (end of 8th century to the 10th century) sumō became part of an important and gorgeous ceremony (*sumō-sechié*) held at the Imperial Court.

Edo *Kanjin-zumō*

With the rise of *bushi* (warrior) society, sumō was used as a martial art to discipline both mind and body. The Edo period (17th to 19th centuries) saw a tranquil period free of war and strife, so sumō developed into a popular form of entertainment with groups of professional sumo wrestlers. *Kanjin-zumō* ("benefit sumō", performed to raise money for the construction and repair of Shintō shrines and Buddhist temples) became popular, especially in the 18th and 19th centuries.

Star *Rikishi* of the Edo Period

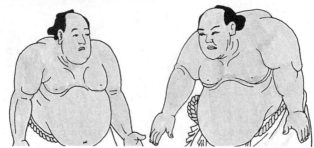

Around the end of the 18th century bouts between the two rival grand champions (*yokozuna*) Tanikazé and Onogawa had the people of the city of Edo going crazy. Starting in 1778 Tanikazé remained unbeaten for four years, with a record of 63 straight victories, until Onogawa defeated him in 1782.

Changing Styles in the Loincloth

In the sumō ceremonies of the Heian period a white hemp *fundoshi* loincloth known as a *tōsagi* was worn. During the *samurai* period *rikishi* wore a hemp cloth dyed red. When benefit sumō became popular, colored silk *mawashi* loincloths were used. In modern days *rikishi* who are ranked *jūryō* (see page 60) or higher wear a silk *mawashi*, and can choose their own color.

Sumō Since the Meiji Period

The Meiji period was ushered in after the age of the *samurai*. The *daimyō*, who had patronized sumō wrestlers, lost their position. This caused a temporary decline in the sport. However, in 1884 the Emperor Meiji attended a sumō bout, and this led to a revival of interest. In 1909 the *Kokugikan* (the stadium for the national sport) was completed, meaning that sumō, which had always been played outdoors, could be performed irrespective of weather conditions. (Prior to this, matches were canceled when the weather was inclement, so that a ten day tournament could be forced to last for one month.)

Sumō is performed in a circular earthen ring called a *dohyō*. (*'Do'* means earth, while *'hyō'* is a long, thin straw sack.) A circle of straw sacking (also called *tawara*), filled with earth and small stones, is embedded in compacted ground. Wrestling is done inside this ring, the diameter of which is fixed.

Four-colored Tassels
From the four corners of the roof suspended over the *dohyo* hang large tassels made of braided rope. Each tassel is of a different color: green for the east (symbolizing the spring), red for the south (summer), white for the west (fall), and black for the north (winter).

Ō-yané (Suspended Roof)

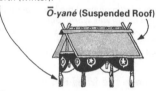

The northern part of the *dohyō* is called the *shōmen* (the front), while the southern part is known as *mukō-shōmen* (opposite the front).

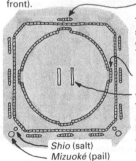

The earthen base of the *dohyō* seen from the side is shaped like a trapezoid. This allows the earth to dry well, and makes for easy viewing. The slope helps break falls.

Toku-dawara

Shikiri-sen

This is the line to guide a wrestler during *shikiri* (see page 35). The line is drawn on the leveled ground using white enamel. The referee will give a warning if the *rikishi*'s hands cross the *shikiri-sen*.

Shio (salt)
Mizuoké (pail)

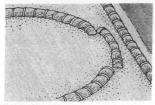

Toku-dawara

Straw sacking (called *tawara*), the same width as that of the ring proper, is embedded just outside the ring at the four points of a compass. This is to assist drainage after a rain (years ago all *dohyō* were outside). Because *toku-dawara* are placed outside the ring circumference, *rikishi* have a slight advantage at these points (*toku* means advantage).

The area outside the ring is swept flat with a broom after each bout, to make it easier to judge whether a foot has strayed into this part.

Changes in *Dohyō* Over Time

Hitokataya Dohyō

Before *tawara* straw sacking was used to define the ring, sumō wrestlers themselves made a circle within which the bout was held. The winner was the person who knocked over his opponent or pushed him down against the human barrier. But this led to many injuries and squabbles.

Early *Dohyō*

In the 17th century the area was delineated by four square columns with rope strung between them. Later long and thin straw sacking filled with earth and small stones enclosed the floor, but in some cases the *dohyō* were square.

RIKISHI APPEARANCE

力士のいでたち

Sumō wrestlers grow their hair long, and tie it up in a *magé* topknot. Their only clothing during a bout is the *mawashi*. This makes for a unique appearance. The topknot was worn by *samurai* in the Edo period, but with the advent of the Meiji period the government ordered ordinary citizens to cut their hair; only sumō *rikishi* were permitted to keep the traditional *magé*.

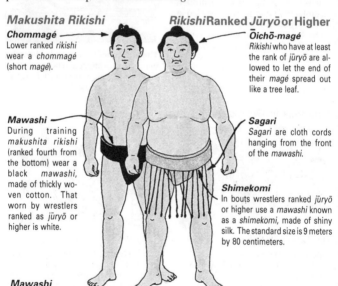

Makushita Rikishi

Chommagé
Lower ranked *rikishi* wear a *chommagé* (short *magé*).

Mawashi
During training makushita rikishi (ranked fourth from the bottom) wear a black *mawashi*, made of thickly woven cotton. That worn by wrestlers ranked as *jūryō* or higher is white.

Rikishi Ranked Jūryō or Higher

Ōichō-magé
Rikishi who have at least the rank of *jūryō* are allowed to let the end of their *magé* spread out like a tree leaf.

Sagari
Sagari are cloth cords hanging from the front of the *mawashi*.

Shimekomi
In bouts wrestlers ranked *jūryō* or higher use a *mawashi* known as a *shimekomi*, made of shiny silk. The standard size is 9 meters by 80 centimeters.

Mawashi

The *mawashi* is made of thickly woven cotton or, for those with at least the rank of *jūryō*, of silk. The cloth itself is flexible, though hard. The *mawashi* protects the inner organs of the wrestler who is naked except for this loincloth. The *mawashi* is also the only handhold an opponent has to grab onto for dear life.

Tying the *Mawashi*

The thick cloth *mawashi*, about 50 centimeters in width and 7 meters in length, is folded and wrapped around the loins. It must be wrapped and fastened quite tightly and firmly, so that it does not become undone during the ensuing struggle.

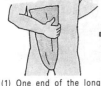 

(1) One end of the long *mawashi*, which has been folded lengthwise in four, is passed between the legs, opened up, folded in two, and made into a *maé-bukuro*. This part is held, covering the front.

(2) Fold the *mawashi* behind the buttocks lengthwise in eight, and secure it with the left hand.

(3) Bring the loose part around from the back, wrap it over the cloth that covers the crotch, and bring it behind again. Repeat.

 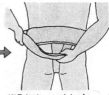

(4) The short loose part covering the front is called the *taté-mawashi*. Bring it down, and wrap the *mawashi* over it once.

(5) Fold the *taté-mawashi* in two, bring it up to the top right-hand side, folding it into a triangular pouch, then wrap the *mawashi* over it once.

(6) Take the remaining free part of the *mawashi* which is behind the body, fold it lengthwise in eight, and pass it under the *taté-mawashi*.

(7) Next, pull it up under the *yoko-mawashi* (horizontal section).

(8) The part you passed under the *yoko-mawashi* will be at an angle. Pass the remaining free end under it.

(9) Pass the remaining part under the right side, and leave it like that. The *mawashi* is now secure.

Keshō-mawashi

The *keshō-mawashi* is a colorful apron hung from the front for the *dohyō-iri* (ring-entering) ceremony (see page 40). When *rikishi* attain the rank enabling them to participate in the *dohyō-iri* ceremony their fan club members present them with this apron.

Yokozuna

Yokozuna is the highest rank a *rikishi* can attain. When a *yokozuna* enters the ring during the *dohyō-iri* he wears a thick braided cord (*tsuna*) made of hemp and bleached cotton hung over his *keshō-mawashi*. This *tsuna* can weigh from 10 to 15 kilograms.

Shikona

Wrestlers' names, known as *shikona*, are sometimes derived from their place of birth, though in many cases the names call to mind the majesty of nature, using Japanese characters which signify, for example, mountains, rivers, or the sea.

Even in the street sumō wrestlers wear *kimono*, even *haori*, not western clothes.

Gyōji Attire

Sumō is refereed by a *gyōji*. The higher his rank, the more gorgeous and elaborate is the embroidery and weave of his costume. We can tell his rank by the color of his *gumbai* fan and cord tassels hanging from his chest.

Taté-gyōji

Eboshi hat

Hitataré attire

Tantō short sword

Zōri sandals

Tabi socks

Gyōji Ranked as Makushita or Lower

Eboshi hat

Hitataré attire

Suashi (bare feet)

Taté-gyōji is the highest rank a referee can attain. Among other matches, he judges the *musubi-no-ichiban* (the last bout of the day).

Gumbai Fan

The *gumbai* is shaped like a gourd or an egg. In either case it is about 25 centimeters long and 20 centimeters wide; the shaft is about 45 centimeters long.

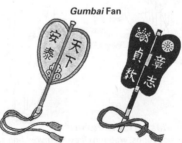

The *gyōji's gumbai* fan is the same type that was first used in the civil war period (around the 16th century) by a warlord when assuming command. The color of the *gumbai's* tassels depends on the *gyōji's* rank.

A SUMŌ MATCH

取り組み

A sumō match is called a *tori-kumi*. In principle only sumō wrestlers who belong to different stables (see page 54) compete against each other. From the moment the *rikishi* are called to the *dohyō* until they withdraw you will see all kinds of rituals and conventions. If you know a little about their origin and meaning you will find the bouts more interesting.

Entrance

Rikishi enter the stadium about 2 matches before their own, and wait their turn in a special place near the *dohyō*. Those who have at least the rank of *jūryō* wait seated on their own special *zabuton* cushion.

The *Yobidashi* (Announcer)

When one bout ends, wooden clappers (*hyōshi-gi*) announce the next. At this signal the next pair of *rikishi* stands up. The *yobidashi* (announcer) holds his white fan at eye level and reads out the names in a theatrical voice. The *rikishi* mounts the *dohyō* when his name is called.

Shiko (Ritual Stamping)

With one leg bent at the knee, the *rikishi* raises his other leg, then brings it down hard. This stamping, called *shiko*, is an important ritual in sumō. It strengthens the lower body, and is a warm-up exercise as well. *Shiko* also shows the *rikishi*'s eagerness to trample on his opponent and to crush any evil that may lurk underneath.

Sonkyo

Sonkyo is a crouching posture signifying respect for one's rival. Hands are placed on the knees, which are far apart, the buttocks rest on the heels, and shoulder muscles are relaxed. The aim here is to steady the nerves and breathing.

Chiri-chōzu

Next the wrestlers conduct a ritual with their hands. They put both hands together, then spread them apart in a small circular motion with their palms up, point them downwards, then move them back to the original position. This polite gesture indicates the *rikishi* are concealing no weapon, and that they are ready to fight fair and square.

Kiyomé-jio

Before the bout the *rikishi* throw salt on the *dohyō*. In Japan since ancient times salt has been regarded as a purifier. The salt in sumō cleanses the *dohyō*, and symbolizes the wish to avoid injury. It also kills germs and helps to harden the dirt.

Chikara-mizu ("water of strength")

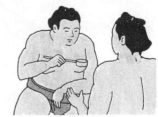

On the *dohyō* the wrestlers receive water brought in a ladle by the *rikishi* who won the previous bout, or by one who is waiting. This water is used to rinse the mouth, and helps to concentrate one's energy. Next the lips are wiped dry with *chikara-gami* ("paper of strength") — this symbolizes a cleansing of the body.

Prize Money Pennants

Different companies and associations offer prize money which will go to the winner (the amount of each prize is fixed). Before the match the announcer makes one turn around the *dohyō* with pennants which display the sponsors' names. If the *rikishi* is popular, and before much-awaited bouts, many prizes are offered, and the crowd rumbles in anticipation.

Shikiri

After the rituals of *shiko*, *sonkyo* and *chiri-chōzu*, it is time for *shikiri*. Each wrestler places his hands on his side of the *shikiri-sen;* each stares at the other, in a moment of judgement. This posture is assumed by both at the same time, practically in the same breath. This is repeated a number of times: the maximum time allowed is 2 minutes for those ranked as *makushita* or lower, 3 minutes for *jūryō*, and 4 minutes for *makuuchi* wrestlers.

Tachiai

While the bout is in progress the *gyōji* may yell out, *"Hakkeyoi nokotta nokotta!"*

The *tachiai* is the moment when both *rikishi* lunge forward from the *shikiri-sen* line. If both men have waited until the end of their allotted time, the *gyōji* will put his fan flat, place it between the pair, and proclaim, *"Matta nashi"* (no time to wait!). Both wrestlers must now place their hands on the ground at the same time and lunge.

Winner and Loser

The outcome is decided in a short period of time. There are 70 ways to win (see page 44) but in actual fact most bouts end in victory after an *oshi* (push), *yori* (grip) or *tsuki* (slap or thrust).

Here are some examples:

(1) During the *tachiai*, one *rikishi* flies at and collides with his rival, his arms bent and his body weight forced against the other (this is the *buchi-kamashi*). He pushes up against the other's chest and chin to throw him off balance (*kachi-agé*). With this same motion he pushes his opponent's chest, forcing him out of the ring (*tsuki-dashi*).

(2) Following the *tachiai* and *buchi-kamashi*, one wrestler grabs his opponent's *mawashi*, then uses the entire mass of his own body to push the other gradually out of the ring (*yori-kiri*).

(3) During the *tachiai* one man takes a lunge at the other. The latter sidesteps, slaps the other on the shoulder or back, causing him to pitch forward and touch his hand on the ground (*hataki-komi*).

Judging

There are a number of ways you can lose:

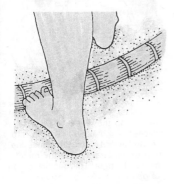

(1) If you are the first person to have any part of your body touch the sand outside the *dohyō*;

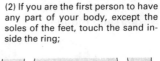

(2) If you are the first person to have any part of your body, except the soles of the feet, touch the sand inside the ring;

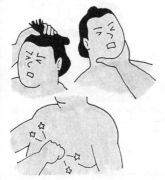

(3) If you use any forbidden technique;

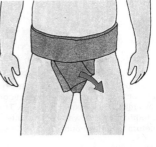

(4) If the *maé-bukuro* part of your loincloth becomes undone.

Naming the Victor

After the end of the bout, the *rikishi* return to their positions. Together with the *gyōji* referee (who is in the middle), they bow once. The *gyōji* recites the name of the victor, and raises his *gumbai* fan in that direction. The winner takes up the *sonkyo* posture, and forcefully moves his right arm horizontally to the right.

Té-gatana o kiru

When prize money is involved, the *gyōji* puts it on his *gumbai* fan and offers it to the winner. The *rikishi* places his right hand out, palm vertical, and jerks it as if to cut something, first to the left, then to the middle, then to the right. This gesture, called *té-gatana o kiru*, symbolizes his thanks to the three gods of victory.

Mizu-iri and *Mono-ii*

If the bout lasts more than a certain period of time, or if there is no obvious outcome in view, the ringside judges may signal the *gyōji* to interrupt the struggle: this is called *mizu-iri*. The wrestlers take a break and rinse their mouths with the "water of strength". They then assume the same postures as before the interruption, and continue from there.

Mono-ii (literally, 'to say something') occurs when the judges disagree with the *gyōji*'s decision. In this case the judges confer in the ring before coming to a decision. Nowadays they also make use of video recordings.

The victor remains near the ring, to present a ladle of water to the next contestants. The underlying meaning here is to wish the *rikishi* the same luck he had. The loser is given water by the next wrestlers who are waiting.

The *hana-michi* (literally, 'flower path') is the walkway from the wrestlers' room (*shitaku-beya*) past the audience's seats to the *dohyō* in the center. During the *sumō-sechié* ceremony (see page 23) in the Heian period *rikishi* would put imitation flowers in their hair before they made their appearance, hence the name *hana-michi*.

Yumitori-shiki

After the last bout of the day a ceremony named *yumitori-shiki* (receiving the archer's bow) is performed on the *dohyō*. In the old days a long bow was presented to the victor of the *musubi-no-ichi-ban* (the last bout of the day) fought on the *senshūraku* (the last day of a 15-day tournament). Part of the ceremony was the victor twirling the bow. To make modern-day matches more entertaining this ceremony is performed at the end of every day.

After the *makushita* and *jūryō* divisions finish their matches, *makuuchi* wrestlers divide into east and west, then all mount the *dohyō* wearing their *keshō-mawashi*. This is the colorful *dohyō-iri* ceremony. The names of wrestlers waiting in line on the *hana-michi* are called out one by one. They mount the platform to the applause of the audience. The sight of so many *rikishi* assembled in full strength around the *dohyō* is a highlight of the day.

The *rikishi* clap their hands to signify their purity before the gods, and the *gyōji* referee assumes a *sonkyo* posture in the middle of the circle.

In ancient times the *rikishi* would all perform the *shiko* stamping ritual, then posture with their hands on their chests (this is still done by *yokozuna* — see the next page). Nowadays, though, since so many wrestlers appear at one time, this ritual has been shortened to everyone simply lifting their *keshō-mawashi* a little, and raising their arms high. These gestures indicate their vow to the god of the *dohyō* to fight fairly, without weapons.

Yokozuna Dohyō-iri

The *dohyō-iri* ceremony of the *yokozuna*, the grand champion, is worthy of his strength and prowess. After the *makuuchi* wrestlers have finished their ceremonial entrance, the *yokozuna*, decorated with his *keshō-mawashi* and *tsuna* (large white cord), and accompanied by a *tsuyu-harai* ("dew remover") and *tachi-mochi* (sword bearer), mounts the *dohyō*. The sight of the *yokozuna* stamping his feet and raising his arms high is most impressive.

The *Tachi-mochi*
The *yokozuna*'s long sword (a symbol of the champion's prowess) is carried by the *tachi-mochi*. He too is a *makuuchi* wrestler and a member of the same stable.

The *Tsuyu-harai*
The *tsuyu-harai*, who is a *makuuchi* wrestler from the same stable as the grand champion, precedes him into the stadium.

There are two ways the *yokozuna dohyō-iri* can be performed. In the *unryū* style, the grand champion places his left hand on his chest, thrusts out his right, and rises up. However, in the *shiranui* style, he spreads both arms and rises as if he is gathering something in them.

PRESENTATION OF AWARDS AND PARADE

表彰式とパレード

On the *senshūraku* (the last day of the tournament) all winners and those meriting commendation are honored in an award ceremony, after which they ride in an open car parade to their own stables (or to the stable they are using when the tournament is held elsewhere).

The names of successive victors are engraved on the cup.

The *makuuchi* winner receives the Emperor's cup and the victor's pennant.

Large photographs of winners are exhibited in the *Kokugikan* sumō stadium.

There are additional prizes to honor extraordinary distinction, fighting spirit, and special skill. These prizes are awarded to *rikishi* from among those in the *makuuchi* rank (other than *yokozuna* and *ōzeki*) who won at least eight bouts.

Other Prizes

In addition to the victor's cup and pennant, many other kinds of prizes are given by sponsors. Here are some examples:

Prize money

One year's supply of gasoline

10,000 bars of soap

A cow

30 bales of rice

A truckload of vegetables

An automobile

1000 shiitaké mushrooms

1500 liters of orange juice

10,000 eggs (boiled in hot spring water)

1 ton of shellfish

1 ton of plums

1 year's supply of cola

Victory Parade

Rikishi, wearing *hakama* adorned with their crests, are feted in an open car parade, bathed in the cheers of thousands of fans.

After they return to their stables they are surrounded by their supporters and celebrate their victory with saké drunk from huge *sakazuki* (saké cups).

WINNING TECHNIQUES

相撲の技

Sumō techniques used to overcome an opponent are called *kimari-té*. A long time ago *kimari-té* numbered 48, divided into four groups of 12: *nagé-waza* (throwing), *kaké-waza* (tripping), *sori-té* (throwing over), and *hineri-té* (twisting). The end of the 19th century (middle of the Meiji period) saw the addition of other techniques used to throw one's opponent out of the ring. The Japan Sumō Association currently recognizes a total of 70 *kimari-té*.

Oshi-dashi

Place your hands on your opponent's chest or under his armpits, lower your center of gravity, then push him upward and out of the ring.

Tsuki-dashi

Thump your palms hard against his chest doing *tsuppari* (slapping and thrusting), then push him out of the ring.

Yori-kiri

Both of you have your arms under the armpits of the other (*yotsu-mi*). Grab his *mawashi*, twist and push him to make him lose his balance, then toss him out of the ring.

Okuri-dashi

When your opponent has his back or side to you, push or jab him out of the ring.

Utchari

Here you turn tables on your opponent, who has come at you hard and pushed you to the very edge of the ring. Lower your hips, raise him up on your belly, bend backward, twist to one side, and toss him out of the ring.

Tsuri-dashi

Grab his *mawashi* with both hands, lift him off the ground and carry him out of the ring.

Uwaté-nagé

Pull his *mawashi* with the hand of your upper arm (the one that is above his during *yotsu-mi*), then drop him as you pull him towards you.

Shitaté-nagé

Pull his *mawashi* (using the hand of your arm that is under his during *yotsu-mi*), then throw him down.

Koté-nagé

After your opponent has his arm under your armpit, grip it with your own upper arm. Use this grip and his own force to throw him. The interesting point here is you do not hold his *mawashi*.

Sukui-nagé

Here again you do not grip his *mawashi*. Place your arm under his armpit in a kind of hug, and use it to throw him.

Uwaté-hineri

Pull his *mawashi* with your upper arm *(uwaté)*, and twist him down to the ground with it. (If it is your right arm, twist him to the right.)

Shitaté-hineri

Pull his *mawashi* with your lower arm (the one which is under his armpit, *shitaté*) and twist him down to the ground.

Uchi-musō

Grab onto the inner side of his leg with your upper hand, lift it up, then twist your body. His feet leave the ground and he will fall.

Soto-musō

Pull out your arm which was under his armpit, tilt your body to one side and place your palm on the outside of his knee. Grab his hand with your other hand, and twist your body till he loses balance.

Uchi-gaké

Grab his *mawashi*, then thrust one leg inside his legs and around one of them. Lean forward against him, pushing him backwards, then pull his leg and drop him.

Soto-gaké

Grab his *mawashi*, twist your leg around the outside of his, pull him hard and drop him.

Hiki-otoshi

When you are locked together in a vicious struggle, suddenly pull the hand he is using to jab you, then make him drop both hands to the ground.

Maki-otoshi

With one hand in his armpit, rock him to the left or right in a hugging motion, then dump him.

Abisé-taoshi

At the edge of the ring, when he is bent over backward, place your weight on top of him to squash him down.

Tsuki-otoshi

As soon as he grabs your *mawashi* and pulls hard, jab his flank on the outer side, move his center of gravity sideways, then drop him.

Kawazu-gaké

Twist one of your legs around the inside of one of his. At the same time put his head under your arm. Jump forward, pulling his leg with yours, thereby making him fall backward.

Mitokoro-zemé

Twist your leg around either the inside or outside of one of his. Get a hold on his other leg (from either the inner or outer side), raise it up, then thrust him away from you.

Kimé-dashi

After he has an arm under your armpit, squeeze so that he cannot move the joint. With him in this position, push him out of the ring.

Kata-sukashi

When you are grappling with each other, and as soon as he moves forward, grab his arm with the hand of your arm which is under his armpit, swing your body outward, push his shoulder with your other hand and pull/push him down.

Kubi-nagé

Wrap one arm around his neck and drop him.

Ké-kaeshi

While the both of you are pushing and shoving, reduce his effectiveness by using the sole of your foot to thrust his ankle outward. Pull him at the same time. This should cause him to fall forward and touch one knee on the ground.

Komata-sukui

When he is trying his best to stay upright by moving his feet forward or bending backward, place your free hand on his thigh under the crotch, lift him upward and topple him back.

Nichō-nagé

Wrap one leg around the outside of his knee, make both of his legs lose their balance, then throw him.

Watashi-komi

With the both of you struggling with arms under armpits, pull his knee outward with the hand of your upper arm, then stretch your other arm forward and out. Put the weight of your upper body on him to topple him.

Hataki-komi

When he lunges at you, swing to one side, then bring the palm of your hand down hard on his back or shoulder to slap him down.

Tottari

Attack suddenly from the side, grab the wrist and elbow of one arm, then throw him.

Saka-tottari

When he is trying *tottari* on you, relax your grip momentarily, then pull to retrieve your hand. By so doing you will pull his arm and achieve *tottari* first.

Certain moves are not allowed, being considered dangerous or unfair. A winner will be disqualified if he uses one. (Such moves are very rarely seen in professional sumō.)

The following are strictly forbidden:

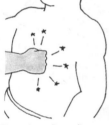

Thrusting a fist or finger into sensitive places such as the eye or solar plexus.

Bending a finger back at the joint.

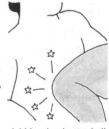

Jabbing the chest or belly with the toes or knee.

Grabbing the throat.

Grabbing the *maé-bukuro* (see page 29).

Grabbing the hair.

Other Forbidden Moves for Amateur Matches:

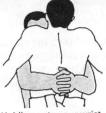

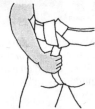

Slapping the face or ear.

Holding onto your wrist or fingers behind his back. If you put your fingers together behind his back the judges will have you change position.

Grasping his *taté-mawashi* (see page 29). Here too the judges will have you change position.

Other Forbidden Moves for Elementary and Junior High Students:

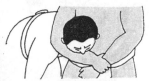

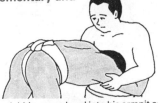

Encircling his neck with your arm.

Jabbing your head into his armpit or into his chest or lower.

Putting your arms around his back and squeezing hard.

Both contestants pushing their heads against the other's chest, then shoving with the neck.

A HARD LIFE IN THE STABLES
相撲部屋

All wrestlers who make sumō their life are attached to a stable called a *sumō-beya*. *Sumō-beya* are managed by a *sumō-toshiyori* (a retired *rikishi* called an *oyakata*). The young wrestler trains here under the guidance of this stablemaster and his seniors. The stable is also his home.

Examination

Height (minimum 173 cm) and weight (not less than 75 kg) are taken, and basic muscle strength is measured.

To enter a *sumō-beya* all applicants must first pass an examination set by the Japan Sumō Association. No one is exempt, not even those who have been scouted by the stables which believe them to be suitable candidates.

Training

The young apprentice first learns the sumō basics. For six months he receives instruction, and gets extra experience during tournaments and sumō tours in various parts of Japan.

Training starts early in the morning. For about two hours each day the *oyakata* and senior apprentices will show him the ropes, especially the basic movements.

Instruction is not only physical: social studies, sports medicine, sumō history and calligraphy are also taught.

Sumō is a sport replete with courtesies and polite formalities, so drills in etiquette are conducted most severely.

Sumō Exercises

Training is what life in the stables is all about. It begins early in the morning with novices awake at 5. First they prepare the instruction ring and do warm-ups. The training is unique to sumō, since wrestlers, in addition to needing excellent reflexes, must be able to push inexorably forward inch by inch, and have the muscular strength to resist and defeat others.

Shiko

We discussed *shiko* previously (page 33). As a basic sumō exercise it strengthens the muscles of the lower half of the body, and provides skill in balancing. The stretching makes the body supple.

First, legs are placed straight out, three foot lengths apart. The buttocks are lowered and hands rest on the knees.

Next, the center of gravity is shifted to one leg, to allow the other one to be raised. Both legs stretch out. Then, the leg in the air comes thumping down, toes touching the ground first, with the knee at about a right angle.

Koshi-wari

Koshi-wari is designed to flex and strengthen the legs and to loosen the hip joints. Legs are opened straight out and the novice squats. From this position he gradually forces his pelvis as low as possible.

Suri-ashi

This leg exercise is unique to sumō. Legs are opened straight out and the trainee squats to a half sitting position, body weight resting on the inside of the legs. The feet then shuffle forward, never leaving the ground.

Teppō

During a bout the opponent may very well make an onslaught. *Teppō* trains one to block him, and strengthens the muscles of the legs, loins, and arms. Novices stand one meter from a pillar or wall. In a coordinated, repetitive motion, left hand and left foot (then the right ones) come forward at the same time. The arm is bent at the elbow at first, then stretched straight out as body weight is applied to the pillar or wall.

Mata-wari

This is another exercise to make the hip joints (indeed, the entire body) supple, and to strengthen the lower body and pelvic area. The trainee sits on the ground and opens his legs wide with knees straight. He forces his torso forward, trying to touch his chest to the ground.

In collision exercises the forehead is pushed against the opponent's chest, and one leg is thrust far forward; then a roll is accomplished.

Ukemi

This exercise is important for all sports involving grappling. Round the body, then roll, using the arms, shoulders and back. The head is placed between the arms so as not to touch the ground. This gives good training in protecting the head and neck, and in softening blows to the bones and joints.

A Day in the Life of an Apprentice

The *sumō-beya* may sleep 4 or 5 in a small room, or 40 to 50 in a large one. This is basically a world of men, all life being conducted by and for men. The novices at the bottom of the ladder do all the work, from preparing meals to running errands for their seniors.

All wrestlers from apprentices to the rank of *makushita* lay down their *futon* bedding in the common room to sleep. Those who have achieved the rank of *jūryō* have their own private rooms, and will be served instead of serving others.

Novices wake early, prepare the *dohyō* for training, and do their warm-up exercises.

The *sekitori* (those with a rank of at least *jūryō*) begin their practice at about 8 o'clock. Apprentices pick up skills by watching them nearby.

Food

Novices must also shop for groceries for all occupants in the stable, after planning the day's menu.

Novices also do the cooking. The meal, one special feature of sumō life, is mainly *chanko-nabé*, food cooked in cauldrons (see page 61). The first meal is eaten only after the morning practice. Seniors eat first, apprentices last. (Seniors are looked after in many ways by apprentices, the latter playing an important role as *tsukibito* servants.)

The nap after the meal is one way *rikishi* can gain and keep the weight they need.

The *oyakata's wife* is called "okami-san" (literally, 'landlady'). She oversees the meals and life in general. In a sense she is the mother of all wrestlers living in the stable.

Climbing Up the Ranks

Winning counts in the world of sumō. Trouncing others regularly could lead to being promoted from apprentice to a much more senior position, leap-frogging several ranks, while losing often may force the man down a rung. In each sumō tournament (called *basho*) those ranked *jūryō* or higher compete in the full 15 bouts; others fight 7 matches. Promotion is considered if the higher ranks win at least 8 of their matches and the lower ranks win 4 or more.

Sumō Ranks

(Both rows, east and west, have the same ranking system.)

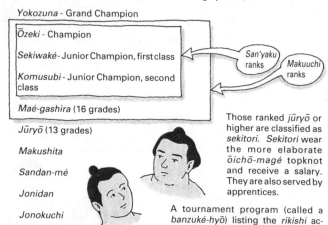

Yokozuna - Grand Champion

Ōzeki - Champion

Sekiwaké - Junior Champion, first class

Komusubi - Junior Champion, second class

San'yaku ranks

Makuuchi ranks

Maé-gashira (16 grades)

Jūryō (13 grades)

Makushita

Sandan-mé

Jonidan

Jonokuchi

Those ranked *jūryō* or higher are classified as *sekitori*. *Sekitori* wear the more elaborate *ōichō-magé* topknot and receive a salary. They are also served by apprentices.

A tournament program (called a *banzuké-hyō*) listing the *rikishi* according to rank makes it easy to see who is who.

Bringing the Good News

Once the Japan Sumō Association decides a *rikishi* is to be promoted to *ōzeki* or *yokozuna*, it sends an official to his room to inform him. The *rikishi*, in the full attire of *mon-tsuki hakama* adorned with his own crest, accepts the promotion and says, *"Kongo mo gambarimasu"* ('I'll keep doing my best.')

Chanko-nabé

Chanko-nabé, the regular fare of *rikishi*, is now famous. There are two varieties, both designed to make and keep one heavy. The first is *Mizu-taki*. The soup stock is brewed without flavoring, though the morsels are dipped into seasoning just before eating. In the case of *Soppu-daki*, the broth is flavored with soy sauce while cooking.

What goes into the pot depends on the stable and the season.
Here are some sample ingredients:

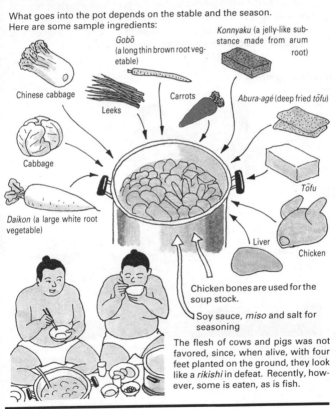

Gobō (a long thin brown root vegetable)

Konnyaku (a jelly-like substance made from arum root)

Chinese cabbage

Leeks

Carrots

Abura-agé (deep fried *tōfu*)

Cabbage

Tōfu

Daikon (a large white root vegetable)

Liver

Chicken

Chicken bones are used for the soup stock.

Soy sauce, *miso* and salt for seasoning

The flesh of cows and pigs was not favored, since, when alive, with four feet planted on the ground, they look like a *rikishi* in defeat. Recently, however, some is eaten, as is fish.

IN RETIREMENT

引退

Rikishi retire when faced with the realization that their age and physical strength no longer enable them to give honor to their present ranking. A special ceremony (*intai hana-zumō*) is held to commemorate the retirement of those ranked *makuuchi* and higher, and their topknot is cut off in the ritual *dampatsu-shiki*.

Dampatsu-shiki

In many cases wrestlers can be seen crying at the *dampatsu-shiki*.

Those going into retirement lose their *magé* (one mark of a sumō wrestler) and wear their hair in the ordinary fashion. In the *dampatsu-shiki* ceremony the *rikishi* sit on the *dohyō* wearing *mon-tsuki hakama* formal attire. Important personages and seniors cut off some of his hair, little by little. But it is the *oyakata* of his stable who cuts off the *magé*.

After retirement many options are open, but most of those who achieved a considerable reputation as *makuuchi* or higher will become *sumō-toshiyori* (*oyakata*) and will train newcomers. At the present time more than 100 *sumō-toshiyori* run their own stables. Not all *sumō-toshiyori* do so, of course, though this option is open to them.

Not all *oyakata*, of course, have their own stable, but some become coaches there.

Other famous retired *rikishi* become sumō commentators for the mass media.

Oyakata also serve as judges during tournaments.

Others may even leave the world of sumō altogether, and open their own *chanko-nabé* restaurant.

ENERGY A TOURNAMENT

ENJOYING A TOURNAMENT
大相撲観戦

In addition to attending one of the six annual sumō tournaments, you may have the opportunity to watch matches when the *rikishi* tour around Japan or overseas, or when they wrestle in competitions sponsored by television stations. You could watch the game on TV, but nothing is better than a seat in the stadium, especially near the action.

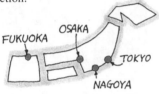

The six *hon-basho* (tournaments) are held in a number of cities in Japan throughout the year: Tokyo in January, May and September, Osaka in March, Nagoya in July and Fukuoka in November. They start on the second Sunday of the month, and last for 15 days.

The atmosphere gets tense the moment the crowd sees the banners lined up in front of the stadium. The banner background is dyed, with the characters indicating the names of the *rikishi* and their *oyakata* left undyed.

A ceremony called the *dohyō-matsuri* is held on the day before the first match of the tournament. To bring good luck things are buried in the middle of the *dohyō*, such as chestnuts, sea-weed, dried squid, rice and salt. Sacred saké is sprinkled in the four corners to ask the gods to prevent injuries. And a drum is carried through part of the city to announce the first day's bouts (*furé-daiko*).

Sumō-jaya (*Kokugikan* Services Co., Ltd.)

The *sumō-jaya* is the agency selling seat tickets (especially for *masu-seki*). It will also deliver drinks, food, and souvenirs to your seat. All people working at the *sumō-jaya* are men.

Masu-seki

These are special seats near the ring side, boxes in which usually four people sit on *zabuton* cushions on the floor. Many people relax here watching bouts while drinking saké and eating. An excellent place to get wrapped up in the excitement of the game, but tournament tickets are very difficult to obtain.

Souvenirs

People holding tickets in the *masu-seki* section will receive large paper bags filled with all kinds of souvenirs (such as beverages, food, pamphlets, schedules of the matches, and ceramic ware).

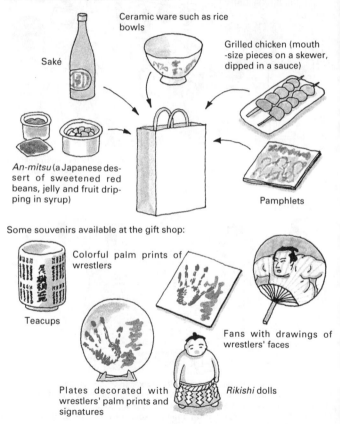

Ceramic ware such as rice bowls

Saké

Grilled chicken (mouth -size pieces on a skewer, dipped in a sauce)

An-mitsu (a Japanese dessert of sweetened red beans, jelly and fruit dripping in syrup)

Pamphlets

Some souvenirs available at the gift shop:

Colorful palm prints of wrestlers

Teacups

Fans with drawings of wrestlers' faces

Plates decorated with wrestlers' palm prints and signatures

Rikishi dolls

Sumō-nishiki-é

Nishiki-é are colored woodblock prints that have their origin in the Edo period. Prints depicting sumō were very common at the time, but declined in popularity during the Meiji period. Recently, however, they are enjoying a revival, and you can see many such woodblock prints of *yokozuna* and other *rikishi* stars at the souvenir shop.

The process involved to make a *nishiki-é* is laborious:

An artist first makes a rough sketch.

Then a carver carves the outlines on wooden blocks.

Next a printer makes impressions many times, one for each color.

SUMŌ TOURS TO OTHER CITIES

地方巡業

After a *hon-basho* tournament is over, some time is available for sumō tours to other cities. The purpose here is to promote sumō and to discover new talent in the country's regions. *Rikishi* also have a chance to hone their skills and to get in better shape for the next tournament.

Cities with a population of at least 50,000 may be lucky enough to be chosen. In principle, tours last about one month, with one day of matches in each city. The schedule is as follows: Kinki district in the spring, Tōhoku district and Hokkaidō in the summer, Tōkaidō, San'yō, San'in and Shikoku areas in the fall, and Kyūshū after the November tournament in Fukuoka.

These tours bring out the big names, with all *sekitori* (those with at least the rank of *jūryō*) from each stable competing. Everyone trains hard early every morning, so this is an excellent opportunity for young *rikishi* to improve their technique. Many locals gather in the early hours of the morning to watch the practice and the matches.

When the *rikishi* are on tour they perform special side attractions between bouts (shows not seen in the regular tournaments), so the audience has no time to be bored.

Shokkiri

Shokkiri is the first competition, to determine the victor of two out of three rounds. To liven up the performance wrestlers will spit water on their rivals and entangle the referee.

Tying the Topknot

Another attraction is showing how the topknot is tied. The *rikishi* sits on the *dohyō*. Nimble fingers set to work.

The hair is well lubricated with oil.

All of the hair is pulled back hard and fastened with a cord.

Next the *magé* is tied.

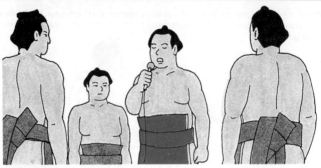

Sumō-jinku

Sumō wrestlers, decorated in their *keshō-mawashi*, stand on the *dohyō* and sing lively traditional folk songs. These are *sumō-jinku*, songs passed down from the end of the Edo period (first part of the 19th century). Lyrics contain references to famous spots and local specialties in Japan, and are interspersed with a rhythmic chant: *"Haa – Dosukoi – Dosukoi!"*

Akeni

This is the box containing objects belonging to wrestlers ranked *jūryō* or higher, such as *shimekomi* (worn during matches) and *keshō-mawashi*. When on tour wrestlers often let this box be seen by the public.

Chanko-nabé Outdoors

On tour the *rikishi* may eat their *chanko-nabé* outdoors. Here fans have a chance to watch them relaxing, something rarely seen during tournaments.

JŪDŌ

柔道

A SHORT HISTORY OF JŪDŌ
柔道の歴史

Jūdō is a refined form of the much older Japanese martial art, jūjutsu. Jūjutsu, a method of self-defense and attack using bare hands or a short weapon, was developed into jūdō by Jigorō Kanō. Jūdō is now popular worldwide, and has even been elevated to the status of an official Olympic sport.

Before Jūdō

It is said that ancient sumō wrestlers grappling without weapons provided the basic inspiration for jūjutsu techniques. Sumō was performed as a solemn ceremony in the aristocratic Heian period (8th to 12th centuries).

In the later military period jūjutsu developed on the battlefield. Soldiers fought unarmed or with a small weapon in hand-to-hand combat. This offensive and defensive military art of throwing or pinning one's opponent became known as jūjutsu.

The Edo period (17th through 19th centuries) saw a period of relative peace, and it was during this time that jūjutsu became a martial art used for training the warrior class. Many different jūjutsu styles were developed (such as *Takenouchi, Tsutsumihōzan, Araki, Sekiguchi, Kitō,* and *Tenjinshin'yō*).

Jūdō Beginnings

Jigorō Kanō added his own special techniques to the various schools of jūjutsu he had studied. In 1882 he established in Tokyo a *dōjō* which he called *Kōdōkan Jūdō*. This first *dōjō*, under the roof of the main sanctuary of Eishō-ji temple, started out with nine students.

The main goal of jūjutsu is the mastery of offensive and defensive techniques. Kanō adapted this goal, but put more emphasis on teaching and learning. He developed three specific aims for jūdō: physical training, improvement of the spirit, and competition in matches.

Jigorō Kanō

Kanō was born in 1860, in what is now Hyōgo Prefecture, just west of Ōsaka. Though always good at academic work, he was frail physically. To overcome this he began to study jūjutsu right after being admitted to Tokyo University in 1877. He gained experience in a number of different styles, and came to the realization that jūjutsu was not just a collection of exercises to be practiced, but also an excellent way to develop one's physical and spiritual powers. In 1882, at the youthful age of 21 only one year after graduation, he set up his own *dōjō*, the *Kōdōkan*.

Kanō's entire life was dedicated to education: after graduating from Tokyo University he became a lecturer at Gakushūin University, after which he held the post of rector at Tokyo Normal School for 26 years. Also, as the founder of the Japan Amateur Sports Association (its present name), he greatly expanded the scope of physical education and sports.

Differences Between Jūjutsu and Jūdō

A literal translation of the word 'jūdō' could be 'the gentle way'. 'Way' here has both an ethical and philosophical connotation. Kanō expressed his philosophical concept with two phrases, "Seiryoku Zen'yō" (efficient use of energy) and "Jita Kyōei" (advantage both for oneself and for others). These maxims stress the importance of using one's physical and mental prowess effectively in everything one does, of respecting others and cooperating with them, and of improving oneself and others in order to bring about a better world.

Jūjutsu, for its part, literally means 'the gentle skill'. Jūjutsu training centered on fixed, formal exercises (kata). Jūdō, however, places stress on randori (the free practice of certain techniques in free-style fighting). This made jūdō training much more dynamic.

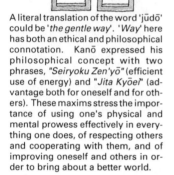

Jūjutsu contestants wore a cumbersome hakama. Early practitioners of jūdō wore a type of short trouser, but they soon adopted certain advantages of functional western clothing to allow for easier movement. Jūdō's present unique uniform (jūdōgi) was developed in 1907.

Jūjutsu techniques, in addition to throws and holds, uses jabs, kicks, and even grappling with small weapons. On the other hand, jūdō avoids dangerous jabs and kicks, concentrating instead on an organized system of throws and defenses (see page 88).

Women's Jūdō

Women were first admitted into jūdō in 1893 (at a time when the place of women in Japanese society was considered far removed from the world of sport). This dramatic innovation was tempered, though, by the fact that women were still kept out of matches, to protect them physically.

After World War II jūdō, for both men and women, was promoted outside Japan as well. The European Jūdō Union was formed in 1948, followed by the establishment of the International Jūdō Federation in 1951. Jūdō became an officially recognized sport for the Olympics when the Games were held in Tokyo in 1964. Women *jūdō-ka* were first recognized in the Olympic Games in Barcelona in 1992.

(When discussing techniques in this book we use the male pronouns *he*, *his*, *him*, though of course it is understood that many women are bringing honor and distinction to the sport.)

Jūdō Ranks and Belt Colors

Above the *shoshinsha* class (initiate) is the bottom rank, 5th *kyū*. From there one advances to 4th *kyū*, etc., up to 1st *kyū*. Number order then

reverses: after *sho-dan* (first *dan*), one is promoted to 2nd *dan*, 3rd *dan*, etc., as high as 10th *dan*. Belt color indicates the *dan* or *kyū*. Novices, 5th *kyū* and 4th *kyū* wear a white belt; brown is for 3rd, 2nd and 1st *kyū*. A black belt can be worn by those with a *dan*, from *sho-dan* to 5th *dan*. Holders of the 6th to 9th *dan* wear a checkered red and white belt, though at times wear a black belt instead. The top rank, 10th *dan*, is recognized with a red and white belt. Women who have achieved the *dan* stage have a white line running through the middle of their black belt.

Jūdō matches are held in a square area covered with *tatami* mats. In addition to the mats, most jūdō *dōjō* now have springs under a false floor, to soften falls.

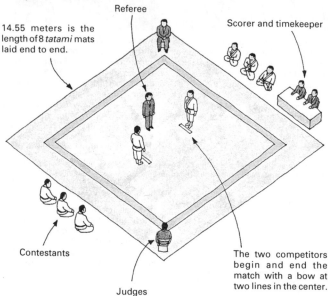

Referee

Scorer and timekeeper

14.55 meters is the length of 8 *tatami* mats laid end to end.

Contestants

Judges

The two competitors begin and end the match with a bow at two lines in the center.

Matches are held in the *jō-nai*, the area delineated by (and including) the red dividing line. The area contains 50 mats, and is 9.1 meters square. *Waza* techniques performed in the area outside the dividing line (*jō-gai*) are invalid.

The Uniform

The loose-fitting *jūdōgi* must be the correct size for the contestant.

Belt
The belt is long enough to leave 20 to 30 cm protruding from each side of the knot when tied.

Naka-sodé

Sodé-guchi

Trousers
The trousers are also loose-fitting: a space of 5 to 8 cm exists between the leg and the trouser leg. Length is a little more than two-thirds the distance from the knee to the ankle.

Yoko-eri

Maé-eri

Maé-obi

Suso-guchi

Jacket
The bottom of the jacket covers the buttocks when the belt is tied.

There is a 5 to 8 cm space between the sleeves and the entire length of the arm. The end of the sleeve comes a little more than two-thirds of the way down the length of the forearm.

Putting on the Uniform

Trousers

The holes for the waist string and the kneepads show you which is the front.

Jacket

Left lapel goes over the right one.

Tying the Belt

Place the middle of the belt in front of you.

Bring both sides behind you and around in front again.

Bring the two ends together, passing one end under and up.

Make the knot ends start out horizontally. Tie the knot tightly so it will not become undone.

CONTESTS AND RULES

競技法とルール

Jūdō matches are held between individuals and between teams. Some competitions are divided into 8 categories, depending on body weight. Others are fought according to *dan,* age or other considerations. And some make no distinction whatsoever.

Jūdō is conducted with every courtesy throughout, so both contestants bow politely to each other at the beginning and end of the bout.

Beginning

Contestants face each other, align their toes with their respective lines, and stand upright.

They bow to each other from the waist at the same time.

They move forward one pace, starting with the left foot.

Both stand in the *shizen hon-tai* natural posture (see page 83). The referee announces *"Hajimé"* ('Begin!') to start the contest.

End

Both contestants return to their lines in the middle of the competition area, then stand in the *shizen hon-tai* posture.

The referee announces the result of the match.

Contestants move back one pace, starting with the right foot.

They bow to each other, then leave the floor.

Before the match, the time to be allowed is fixed at 3 to 20 minutes. The winner is the first contestant to obtain one point, by performing a *nagé-waza* (throwing) or *katamé-waza* (pinning). If the outcome cannot be decided within the allotted time, the superior player wins or the bout ends in a draw.

***Ippon* (One Point)** You can receive one point with either of the following:

* *Nagé-waza*: When you throw your opponent, or when you overcome his technique and throw him on the back, with considerable force and speed.

* *Katamé-waza*: When your hold makes him give up, saying *"Maitta!"* (I give up), or tapping twice with his hand or leg. Or, for example, when you hold him (*osaé-waza*) for 30 seconds after the announcement, "osaekomi".

***Waza-ari* (Half Point)** You will be awarded a half-point with:

* *Nagé-waza*: When the technique was almost good enough to receive a full point.

* *Katamé-waza*: When one contestant holds the other for at least 25 seconds.

If one contestant receives two *waza-ari* he receives a total of one point (*waza-ari-awaseté-ippon*).

Receiving a *Yūkō*

* *Nagé-waza*: When a technique was almost good enough to receive one *waza-ari*.

* *Katamé-waza*: When one contestant holds the other for at least 20 seconds.

If you have only one *waza-ari* you are not entitled to a win, no matter how many *yūkō* you have received.

Prohibited Moves

No dangerous *waza* or moves are allowed. There are a total of 31 (32 for women) actions which are forbidden. Players will be given one of four different warnings (*shidō*, *chūi*, *keikoku* or *hansoku-maké*), depending on the extent of the infringement.

Shidō

This is a warning for a small violation of the rules. The match is interrupted, and both contestants return to their starting lines. An *'awaseté-chūi'* is applied to a wrongdoer the second time.

Here are some examples of when this warning is given:

If you obviously lose your fighting spirit and make no attack for at least 30 seconds;

If you insert a finger or fingers inside the bottom end of his sleeve or trouser leg, then hold on. Or, in a standing position, when you grasp onto and twist the end of his sleeve;

In a standing position, if you use your fingers to interlock with his, for at least 6 continuous seconds;

If you disarray his *jūdōgi* or retie your own belt, etc., without the referee's permission;

If you encircle the end of your belt (or the bottom of your jacket) once around his arm;

If you put any part of his *jūdōgi* in your mouth;

If you put any part of your limbs directly on his face, or if you pull his hair.

80

Chūi

Here are a few infringements which call for *chūi*. (The contest will be interrupted, with both returning to their starting position.)

If you put a foot or leg inside his belt, lapel or collar during a *katamé-waza* hold;

If you bend his fingers back to break his grip;

If you kick his arm with your knee or foot to break his grip.

If you have been warned with a *shidō*, the second slight infringement could warrant a *chūi*. In judging, a *chūi* has a reverse value the same as a *yūkō*.

Keikoku

This, like *hansoku-maké*, is a serious penalty, and is warranted:

 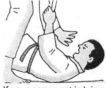

If you apply a *kansetsu-waza* (joint lock) anywhere other than to the elbow.

If your opponent is lying face up on the mat, and you lift his body up, then drive it back to the mat.

If you perform any movement which is dangerous to your opponent or which goes against the spirit of jūdō.

Once you have been warned with a *chūi*, the second slight or serious infringement warrants a *keikoku*. A *keikoku* has a reverse value the same as a *waza-ari*.

Correct posture is important in jūdō. If you master the fundamental standing, walking and defensive postures, your body will move just as you desire. And since you will grapple a great deal with your opponent, it is important that you learn the basic elements of grappling and falling.

First of all, *Seiza*

From a standing position, move your left foot back, then place your left knee on the ground where your left toes were. Do the same with your right knee, then place your legs and feet together. (At this stage your toes are still upright on the floor.) Straighten your toes, letting the tops of your feet rest on the ground, and rest your buttocks on your heels. This is the *seiza* position. When standing up, follow the opposite procedure in the reverse order (i.e. starting with the right).

Salutations

Expert contestants always respect their opponents and remain calm. The bows in jūdō express this respect and composure.

***Ritsurei* (standing salutation)**
Stand to attention with your heels together. Bend your upper body forward about 30 degrees. Hands are in front of your legs. Remain still in this position a moment, then return to your previous standing position.

***Zarei* (kneeling salutation)**
In the *seiza* position, with back straight and chin pulled in, bend your upper body forward, placing both hands apart on the floor with fingers pointing somewhat inward. Remain still in this position a moment, then return to *seiza*.

Postures

Shizen-tai (basic natural postures)

In the *shizen-tai* you stand in the natural way. From this basic stable position it is easy to change quickly and nimbly to various other postures.

Shizen hon-tai
Spread both heels about one foot length apart, with weight equally on both feet. Face directly forward and relax your shoulder muscles. This is the fundamental and natural jūdō posture.

Migi shizen-tai
From *shizen hon-tai*, move your right foot forward about one foot length.

Hidari shizen-tai
From *shizen hon-tai*, move your left foot forward about one foot length.

Jigo-tai defensive postures

These postures are taken momentarily to defend yourself. Momentarily, because they are difficult to attack from; use them to protect yourself from an opponent's attack, then return to a *shizen-tai*.

Jigo hon-tai
From the *shizen hon-tai* posture, spread your feet further apart, bending your knees to lower your center of gravity.

Migi jigo-tai
From *jigo hon-tai*, take one step forward with your right foot.

Hidari jigo-tai
From *jigo hon-tai*, take one step forward with your left foot.

Holding Methods

Since jūdō specializes in the art of grappling, holding techniques are important. These may vary, depending on your opponent's size and posture, but in many cases you will put one hand on his sleeve, grasping his lapel with the other. In any event, do not grip his jacket too strongly, as you may need your strength for other efforts.

A hold in *migi shizen-tai*.

A hold in *hidari shizen-tai*.

Right to left hold (each contestant using the technique he is best at).

Suri-ashi

The basic walk in jūdō is with the soles sliding over the *tatami*. This ensures stability. Make sure your paces are regular, to keep your center of gravity stable and to enable you to move nimbly in any direction.

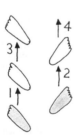 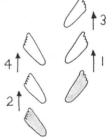

Ayumi-ashi
As in ordinary walking, the legs move forward one after the other.

Tsugi-ashi
In *tsugi-ashi*, make sure the second foot you move does not go past the first one.

Kuzushi

Kuzushi is unbalancing your opponent through pushing, pulling, etc., all the while maintaining your own stability. Once you start shifting his center of gravity you will be better able to follow up with a *waza*.

If you are able to force the other person into an unbalanced position you should be able to accomplish a throw, even if he is bigger and stronger.

Kuzushi can be accomplished in eight basic directions: front, right front corner, right side, right back corner, back, left back corner, left side, and left front corner.

Osaba-hiké
If your opponent pushes you, move back a little, thereby pulling him and throwing him off balance.

Hikaba-osé
If your opponent pulls you towards him, move forward quickly following the direction of his own motion, making him lose balance.

Tai Sabaki (body control)

To perform or change a *waza* you must change body position and/or direction. Here you want to achieve an ideal position or direction, keep your own balance, and make your opponent lose his.

Maé sabaki (front movement control).

Ushiro sabaki (rear movement control).

Achieve an *ō-goshi* (hip roll) from a right leg *maé-mawari sabaki* (front turn control).

Ukemi (break-fall techniques)

By practicing *ukemi* you will be able to protect yourself when you fall or are thrown. Mastering *ukemi* techniques will take away your fear of being tossed around.

Ushiro-ukemi (falling backward)
Feet and legs are together. Raise your legs straight up. Hit the *tatami* hard with the entire length of your arms (palms down) to break your fall. Protect the back of your head by tucking your chin in and curving your back.

Yoko-ukemi (falling sideways)
From a standing position, fall backward, raising one leg, then the other. Bring your right arm up, stretching in front of your face, drop your buttocks to the mat and roll back to the right side, keeping your head off the floor. At the same time, hit the *tatami* with your right arm and palm. Do the same for the left side.

From a squatting position, kick out your right leg diagonally to the left front, drop your right buttock down close to your left heel, and roll back diagonally to the right side, raising both legs and hitting the *tatami* hard with your right arm and hand, palm down. Similar movements can be done for the left side.

Hands are apart, with forearms at a 45 degree angle.

Maé-ukemi (falling forward)

Here you practice protecting the front of your head. Fall forward with both arms in front of you, elbows bent. Fall on your forearms, tighten your stomach muscles, and support your body with your arms and toes.

Maé-mawari ukemi (tumbling forward)

This *ukemi* is very useful if you are thrown. Dropping from the *migi shizen-tai* posture, make a triangle on the mats with your left hand as the apex (fingers pointing in) and your left and right feet forming the base. Push your right shoulder far forward, touching your right palm on the mat with fingers pointing somewhat backward. With your right hand as a fulcrum, kick out your feet and roll forward. Both legs and left arm strike the mat at the same time.

Jūdō techniques can be divided into two broad categories: *nagé-waza* (throwing) and *katamé-waza* (pinning).

(1) *Nagé-waza* can be sub-divided into *tachi-waza* (leg, hip, and hand techniques, all performed while standing) and *sutemi-waza* (body-drop throws, using one's own weight while one is falling oneself);

(2) *Katamé-waza* can be sub-divided into *osaé-waza* (holding techniques), *shimé-waza* (strangle holds using an arm or leg on his neck), and *kansetsu-waza* (joint techniques).

Example of *Nagé-waza*

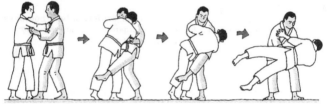

Hiza-guruma (knee whirl)

Bring him off-balance to a front corner. With *maé sabaki* (front movement control), place the sole of your foot on the outside of his knee, and throw him forward in a twisting roll.

Ō-soto-gari (big outside clip)

Bring him off balance to a back corner, with his body practically riding on his right leg. With his and your torsos close together, sweep your right leg back in a large circle, clipping and throwing him.

Ko-uchi-gari (small inside clip)

Make him lose balance straight back or into a back corner, then clip the inside of his right foot with the sole of your foot, raising him up to dump him. The trick here is to clip him the moment his weight comes to bear on his heel.

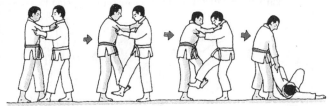

Deashi-barai (forward foot sweep)

The moment he is about to put his weight on the foot he has thrust forward, or the moment he is about to move away (so in both cases his foot is off the mat), sweep his ankle sideways from the outside with the sole of your foot, then drop him.

Uchi-mata (inner thigh reaping throw)

Get him off balance directly to the front, pulling his torso close to yours. Turning away from him, insert your leg between his, and with the outside of your thigh raise up the inside of his thigh and throw him forward.

Ō-goshi (hip roll)

Make him lose balance to the front or a front corner. Swing your arm around to the back of his belt, pulling him closer to you as for a hug. Pivot out so you face away from him, bend your knees, raise him well up on your hip and throw him.

Tsurikomi-goshi (lift-pull hip throw)

Pull him upwards off balance towards the front or into a front corner, at the same time lowering your center of gravity and turning away from him. With your buttocks as fulcrum, throw him forward.

Harai-goshi (hip sweep)

Get him off balance towards the front, pulling him towards your side. Push the back of your hip bone against one side of his lower abdomen, while using your leg to sweep his leg. Then throw him.

Seoi-nagé (shoulder throw)

Off-balance him to the front or a front corner. Bend your knees to lower your center of gravity, all the while pivoting away from him. Pull him up on his toes, then onto your back. Bring him across your shoulder and drop him.

Tai-otoshi (body drop)

Get him off balance in a front corner, then turn away from him, bringing your foot in front of him. Pull his arm hard, and use your leg and hip as fulcrum to pull him over and down in front of you.

Tomoé-nagé (round throw)

Pull him off balance towards you the moment he comes at you, then fall straight back, holding onto him. Use the sole of your foot on his lower abdomen to lift him up and propel him in a flight over your head.

Nagé-waza Combinations

Often you must adapt your own technique to your opponent's defensive posture or aggressive attack. The idea is to cleverly dodge his tactics, at the same time using his own strategies against him. This can be done with these throwing combinations, one *waza* following another.

When You Shift from One Tactic to Another

From right big inside clip to right shoulder throw

Push him backward and off-balance using a right big inside clip. → He pushes against you to avoid falling. → Use his own momentum to pull him hard towards you, then throw him with a right shoulder throw (see page 91).

From right knee whirl to left forward foot sweep

Try a right knee whirl (page 88) on him. → He puts his weight on his left leg, and moves his right leg forward. → At that moment, lower your right foot (which has been on his knee) and use it to support your own weight. Next, accomplish a forward foot sweep (page 89) with your left leg, sweeping his right leg out from under him.

From right big outside clip to right hip sweep

Try a right big outside clip on him from *migi shizen-tai*. → He moves his right leg back, shifting his center of gravity backward to avoid being thrown. → At that instant, with the leg you thrust out (when you tried the outside clip), catch him on his right knee, pivot with your left foot in the direction you want to throw him, then toss him forward in a hip sweep (page 90).

Shifting from His Advantage to Yours

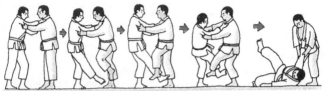

From right forward foot sweep (his effort) to left forward foot sweep (your win)
(See page 89.) He tries a right forward foot sweep on you. → Move your left leg back to avoid his leg, and use this same left leg of yours to sweep his right leg which is sticking out. Drop him with a left forward foot sweep. This is also called a *tsubamé-gaeshi* (swallow flip).

From right small inside clip (his effort) to right round throw (your win)
He pushes towards you, trying a right small inside clip (page 89). → Lift your right leg lightly to avoid his stratagem. → Put this same right leg against his lower abdomen, fall back, and use the resulting force of his being propelled forward to toss him with a right round throw (page 91).

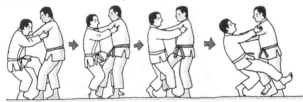

From left round throw (his effort) to right small inside clip (your win)
He tries to make you fly in a left round throw (page 91). Brace him with his right leg, and force him into a backward fall, raising his left leg. → With the same movement, thrust your leg between his legs, and clip his right foot with your right foot, in a right small inside clip (page 89). This should make him fall.

Katamé-waza

Katamé-waza are pinning holds, strangle-holds and joint locks, used to pin your opponent. (*Katamé-waza* techniques are also called *né-waza*, techniques from a lying position.) The basic movements are different from those used to practice *nagé-waza* throws.

Basic Exercises and Movements

Moving on your back
Bend your knees a little. Move forward or backward, using your arms, legs and shoulders. Swivel about with your buttocks as center.

The bridge
Starting lying on your back, arch your body, using only your two feet and the back of your head to support the arch.

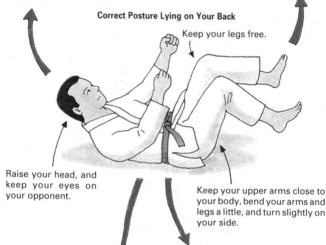

Correct Posture Lying on Your Back

Keep your legs free.

Raise your head, and keep your eyes on your opponent.

Keep your upper arms close to your body, bend your arms and legs a little, and turn slightly on your side.

Pelvic twist
Facing upward, bring one leg over the other, twist your waist and turn to the side.

Leg twirls and stretches
Lying on your back, bend your knees and revolve both legs, one to the inside and one to the outside.
Lie on your back and push out your heels, kicking out one leg, then the other.

Correct Posture on Your Front
When on all fours, rest the weight of your upper body on your elbows, and try always to face your opponent.

Crawling
Face down, with legs outstretched, stretch out your arms and slide forward by bringing your upper arms close to your body.

Leg exercise
When stretched out on all fours, cross one leg under the other, to face a different direction.

Fundamental Attack Patterns
Many *katamé-waza* attacks are performed when your opponent is either face up or face down under you, or when you are on your back under him.

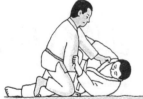

One basic attack pattern when you are above
Drop your right knee to the mat and lower your hips, then get a grip near his knee with your right hand, restraining his knee on the inside of yours. Grip his right lapel with your left hand. Keep your upper body as upright as possible.

One basic attack pattern when you are below
Use your right hand to grab his right lapel from the inside. Your left hand grips the middle of his left sleeve. Pull him towards you with both hands. Push your right foot against his lower abdomen, and hook your left leg around the outside of his right knee.

Examples of *Katamé-waza*

Kesa-gatamé (sash hold)
Get your opponent face up on the mat, then drop your hips, moving in close to his right side. Pin his right arm deep in your left underarm. Bring your right arm around his head and grab his collar at the back. Keep your legs far apart and support part of your weight with your left knee on the mat. Keep him pinned in this hold.

Yoko-shihō-gatamé (side four-corner hold)
Get him face up on the mat. Drop your knees to the mat close to his right side. Slide your left arm under his neck and grab onto his left lapel. Pin his neck with your left shoulder and arm. Thrust your right arm between his legs, grab the side of his belt and pull it towards you, pushing down on his torso with your chest.

Kata-gatamé (shoulder hold)
Have him face up on the mat. Thrust your right knee against his right side on the mat. Use both arms to pull his right arm. Control his head with it. Thrusting your torso forward, slip your right hand in from above his left shoulder, then join your two hands together in the form of a cross. Pin his right arm and neck and complete the hold with head pressure.

Kami-shihō-gatamé (upper four-corner hold)
With him lying face up, approach from above his head, with your knees on the mat. Thrust both of your arms under his arms near the shoulders and grasp both sides of his belt. Clamp both of his arms with your underarms. Drop your torso onto his head and chest and hold him hard.

Kataha-jimé (one-wing strangle)
Move in from behind your opponent.
Slide your right arm over his right
shoulder and grip his left collar.
Thrust your left arm under his left
armpit, bringing up his left arm high
and getting your left arm behind his
neck. Get a strangle hold on him by
applying your left arm and pulling
your right hand.

Okuri-eri-jimé (collar strangle)
Drop your left knee to the mat behind
him. Thrust your left arm under his
left armpit, grab his left lapel and pull
down. Pass your right arm over his
right shoulder in front of his throat
and get a strong grip on his left lapel.
Then change the hold of your left
hand to his right lapel. Press your
torso against him hard and pull back
with both arms, thereby pinning him
in a strangle-hold.

Udé-garami (entangled armlock)
He is on his back. Get close to his
right side. If he tries to grab your
right lapel with his left hand, grab his
left wrist with your left hand from
above. Drop your torso so your chests
come together, and push his left hand
down to the mat. Slip your right hand
under his left arm above the elbow,
and grab your own left wrist from
above. Pull your left arm towards
you, wrenching his left elbow upward with your right arm, thereby
locking his joint.

**Udé-hishigi-jūji-gatamé (arm-taking
cross armlock)**
Again get close to his right side when
he is on his back. If he straightens out
his right arm, grab his wrist with both
hands and pull up. Thrust your right
foot against his back from under his
right upper side, let your upper body
fall forward and bring your left leg
over the top of his head to place it on
his neck. Your buttocks drop down
close to his right shoulder and your
body falls back, so that the two of you
form a cross. This will let you apply
a lock to his elbow.

Katamé-waza Combinations

When You Shift from One Tactic to Another

From sash hold to shoulder hold
(See page 96.) You have him under control with a sash hold. → He wriggles free by twisting his body and pulling his right arm, which you are holding. → As soon as he frees his arm, put your left hand on his right elbow and press it down. Adjust your body position so that you can pin his right arm with the right side of your head, and keep him in a shoulder hold.

From side four-corner hold to arm-taking cross armlock
You have him in a side four corner hold (page 96). → He is trying to escape by twisting to the right. → Adjust your body position to grab his left arm with both hands. Raise your hips and in one swift movement swing your left leg around his head to his left shoulder. Using this leg as pivot, swing around to his left side, restrain his neck with your right leg, and accomplish an arm-taking cross armlock (page 97).

Shifting from His Advantage to Yours

From upper four-corner hold (his effort) to collar strangle (your win)
The intent of his attack is an upper four-corner hold (page 96). → Push up his two shoulders with both hands. Keep holding onto his jacket as you swing around behind him and grab him from behind. Squeeze his torso between your legs, then restrain him with a collar strangle (page 97).

Shifting from *Nagé-waza* to *Katamé-waza*

Even throwing your opponent may not give you the desired one point (*ippon*), but you can follow up your attack with a holding technique.

From shoulder throw to upper four-corner hold

Your shoulder throw (see page 91) was a partial success. → As soon as he is lying on the mat, thrust both arms under his upper arms, grab both sides of his belt, then pin him in an upper four-corner hold (page 96).

From round throw to arm-taking cross armlock

Get ready to toss him in a round throw (page 91). He will struggle against this. → For the throw you have placed your right foot against his lower abdomen. Swing your body around, with that foot as axis, so that your two bodies make the form of a cross. Pull at his right arm, all the while wrapping your left leg over his neck, then pulling at his right arm with both hands to accomplish an arm-taking cross armlock (page 97).

From hip sweep (his effort) to side four-corner hold (your win)

He is trying a hip sweep (page 90) on you but fails and collapses on the mat. → Get in close to his right side, insert your left arm under his head and grab onto his lapel. Pin him in a side four-corner hold (page 96).

JŪDŌ FIRST AID FOR ASPHYXIATION

活法

Jūdō has developed its own special first aid techniques to quickly revive a contestant who has asphyxiated. If your strangle hold was too strong and he has stopped breathing, he needs urgent help.

Lapel Technique

Get behind the unconscious person. Sit on the ground with your right leg stretched out in front and your left leg to the rear. Bend your right knee and push the knee cap against his seventh thoracic vertebra. Grip his right lapel with your right hand and his left lapel with your left. By lifting from this position you will be able to make his chest expand.

With your two hands on his lapels, apply pressure on his chest with one swift movement, making his upper body bend forward. This will cause his lungs to expel air. Next, bend him backward so that he inhales. Keep doing this until he revives.

Hugging Technique

Get him reclining in a semi-sitting position, with you sitting behind him on the ground. Raise up your right knee and have his upper body rest on your chest. Thrust your two arms under his armpits, and place both of your hands, one on top of the other, on his abdomen.

In a kind of lifting, hugging motion, apply pressure with your hands, at the same time bending your body forward, causing him to do the same. His lungs will expel air, starting the breathing function again. Bring him back to the previous position so that he breathes in.

CHAPTER
4

KENDŌ
剣道

Kendō as practiced today is a refined sport, with contestants fencing with bamboo swords, striking, thrusting, parrying, defending and counterattacking. The origins of kendō are lost in time, but the sport surely goes back to the days when men hunted with metal swords.

A Japanese sword

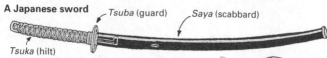

Tsuba (guard) *Saya* (scabbard)

Tsuka (hilt)

A *bushi* from the early period

Early swords, based on Chinese models, were flat and straight, and were worn not so much as weapons but to indicate rank. The sharp, curved Japanese sword, made so strong it would not bend or break, was developed between the time *bushi* (warriors) gained prominence at the end of the Heian period (794-1185) and the Kamakura period (1192-1333). This new weapon led to remarkable advances in swordsmanship.

Tengu teaching martial arts

In the warrior age emphasis was placed on military training, so swordsmanship developed into an art. In the latter half of the Muromachi period (1336-1568) the government lost control, and warfare became common. Swordsmen had ample opportunity on the battlefield, and soon the art of fencing was systematized in a number of different styles.

Legend tells us that the originators of these schools were taught by *Tengu* (a long-nosed wizard) or *kappa* (water sprites).

Some of these written works were in the form of *makimono* scrolls.

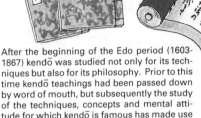

After the beginning of the Edo period (1603-1867) kendō was studied not only for its techniques but also for its philosophy. Prior to this time kendō teachings had been passed down by word of mouth, but subsequently the study of the techniques, concepts and mental attitude for which kendō is famous has made use of written accounts as well.

Musashi Miyamoto

The famous swordsman Miyamoto (1584-1645) was the founder of the *Niten-ichi-ryū* school of fencing, which uses two swords. In his youth he wandered throughout Japan, gaining experience in different combat styles. It is said that his prowess in the use of the spear, *bokutō* (wooden sword) and sickle and chain was so great that he won more than sixty competitions, and never lost one. His duel with Kojirō Sasaki in 1612, in which Sasaki was killed, is now part of the nation's folklore, depicted many times in fiction and the movies. At the age of 60 Miyamoto wrote down his knowledge of military dicipline in *Gorin no Sho* (The Book of Five Rings).

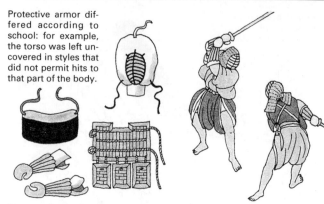

Protective armor differed according to school: for example, the torso was left uncovered in styles that did not permit hits to that part of the body.

From the beginning to the middle of the Edo period emphasis was placed on the study of formal fencing exercises. Bouts between different schools were even forbidden. Aggressive sportsmen, not stimulated by this formalism, developed special protective equipment so they could practice free-style combat.

The Edo period saw a long period of peace. During this time some people were able to buy recognition in kendō techniques, rather than earn it through strict training. As a reaction to such corruption, contests with protective apparel became common, with a view to weeding out rich amateurs.

At the end of the Edo period the Shogunate, weak and ineffectual, was unable to deal with the threat of foreign powers. As a reaction *kenjutsu* (swordsmanship) received increased attention. The practice of sword techniques became popular in *dōjō*, and competitions between contestants wearing armor became common, even between different schools.

Some spectators at these exhibitions were chosen to compete against the swordsmen or against women wielding ax-like weapons.

The Meiji era ushered in a new regime, one not based on *bushi* warriors. Towards the end of the 19th century there was a rush to emulate foreign culture. The study of the ancient techniques of *kenjutsu* fell into steep decline, with swordsmen finding it hard to make ends meet. To earn a living some of them started fencing exhibitions, which proved to be very popular in many parts of the country.

The tips of ancient *shinai* had 32 (not four) strips of split bamboo, covered with a heavy cloth.

With the outbreak of World War I, and in its after-math, kendō was promoted as a Japanese martial art. But this emphasis on military skill prompted the Allies to ban kendō and other military arts after Japan's defeat in 1945.

In 1950, though, kendō specialists developed a new competitive sport based on kendō but using a new version of the *shinai* bamboo sword. Because of renewed interest the All-Japan Kendō Federation was formed. Kendō was reborn, this time as a sport, not as military training.

Words Expressing the Kendō Spirit

Like other martial arts, kendō has developed its own vocabulary, passed down through the centuries in an unbroken line from the original teachers until the present day. These words strike a chord in the hearts of many Japanese people even today.

"Ichi-gan, ni-soku, san-tan, shi-riki"

These list four strategic elements in order: "Eyes first, footwork second, courage third, strength fourth."

"Ken-tai-itchi"

'Ken' means 'to risk' (i.e. to attack), while *'tai'* means 'to wait' (in this case, to protect oneself). This saying tells us that offense and defense are really two sides of the same coin (*'itchi'*): every attack needs a defence, every defence is an offensive tactic as well.

"Zanshin"

Zanshin ('the spirit remaining') refers to keeping one's presence of mind even after finishing a strategic move, getting ready for the next, always on guard, always aware of one's opponent's movements and intentions.

"Shishin"

Too much concentration on one factor (*shishin*) results in seeing nothing else, in losing the strength one needs for the task at hand.

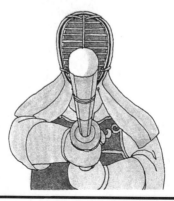

The four emotions to avoid

If we want to win we must avoid four emotions: surprise, fear, doubt and confusion.

"Shu-ba-ri"

Shu-ba-ri are the three stages one passes through to master kendō. First, learn and follow (*shu*) kendō rules and exercises. Next, ignore the exercises (*ba*) and invent techniques which suit you. Finally, move to a higher stage (*ri*) and develop your own strategy in complete freedom.

"Enzan no metsuké"

Metsuké is the point (the part of one's opponent) being observed. Many centuries of study have gone into the tactic of observing the opponent's entire body as one would a distant mountain (*enzan*), all the while closely observing his general strategy.

"San-sappō"

This refers to the three ways to succeed in an attack: render ineffective his defence, surpass his technique, and smother his spirit.

DEFENCE
TECHNIQUE
SPIRIT

EQUIPMENT AND APPAREL
用具と服装

Kendō equipment is most impressive: a bamboo sword (*shinai*) and armor, *keikogi* (jacket) and *hakama* (skirt-like trousers). Feet are bare. Apparel and *shinai* sizes vary greatly, depending on body size.

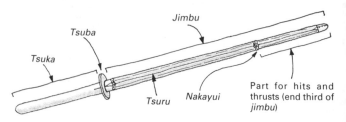

Jimbu

Tsuba

Tsuka

Tsuru   Nakayui

Part for hits and thrusts (end third of *jimbu*)

Shinai

This bamboo sword gets plenty of knocks. It could split, and the strings tying it together could become loose; if it is not looked after well, it could cause an injury.

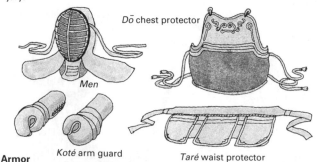

Dō chest protector

Men

Koté arm guard

Taré waist protector

Armor

Kendō armor protects you from your opponent's blows and thrusts, but lets you attack and dodge freely.

Putting on the *Keikogi* and *Hakama*

The *keikogi* (jacket) and *hakama* (skirt-like trousers) are right out of the age of *samurai*. The size must be right, otherwise movement will be impeded.

(1) Put the left side of the *keikogi* over the right, then fasten it with a string on the right side.

(2) Step into the *hakama* and place the front of it against your belly. Bring the front band strings around behind you, then to the front again, and pull them tight.

(3) Take them around to the back again, and tie them together.

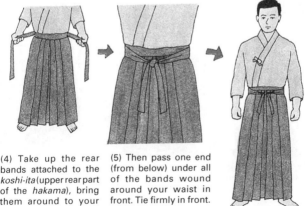

(4) Take up the rear bands attached to the *koshi-ita* (upper rear part of the *hakama*), bring them around to your front, cross them once.

(5) Then pass one end (from below) under all of the bands wound around your waist in front. Tie firmly in front.

Putting on the Armor

The armor must be well-fastened to avoid problems during a bout. It is said that a man's ability can be judged by how he wears his armor.

(1) Place the center of the *taré* (waist and hip protector) against your lower belly, bring the *taré* bands over the bottom of the *hakama*'s *koshi-ita,* then around in front, then tie them under the central *ō-daré*.

(2) Bring the upper left cord of the *dō* chest protector behind then over your right shoulder, pass it through the right loop, and tie. The right upper cord passes over your left shoulder and is tied in the same way.

(3) Bring the lower cords behind you and tie.

(4) Wrap the *tenugui* around the top of your head.

(5) Put on the *men* and tie the cords, with the loose ends hanging down the back less than 40 cm from the knot.

(6) Put on the *koté* arm guards.

Fastening the *Tenugui*

The *tenugui* softens blows landing on your *men,* and serves as a sweat absorber. Here is one way to fasten it:

(1) Rest the *tenugui* on the middle on your head, and hold the two rear corners.

(2) Wrap one corner around to the front and behind again, then the other.

(3) Hold both ends at the back with your fingers.

(4) The front part covers your face. Lift it up.

(5) Tuck it under.

After the Match

Take everything off in the opposite order. The *men* and *koté* are easily damaged by the elements, so store them in a well ventilated place after you have wiped off all perspiration.

(1) Wrap the *taré* strings around the middle *ō-daré* after you smooth out the wrinkles.

(2) Place the *dō* on the *taré.*

(3) Pass the *dō*'s upper cords under, then make a cross in the center. Bring them to the top again and tie.

(4) Securing the *taré*'s *obi* with your hands, wrap the *dō*'s lower cords around, then fasten.

(5) Get the wrinkles out of the leather of the inside of the *koté.*

(6) Place the *men* in the middle of the inside of the *dō,* with one *koté* on each side.

There is nothing more dramatic than a kendō match, with two fencers protected in armor, thrusting and attacking with their bamboo swords. Matches can be held between individuals or between teams. The winner is generally the first person to obtain two out of three points, though one point may be sufficient to win when nobody scores more in the allotted time.

The fencing hall

During a bout contestants must remain within a square marked on the floor, one side of the line being 9 to 11 meters long.

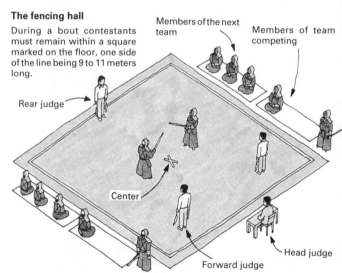

Members of the next team

Members of team competing

Rear judge

Center

Head judge

Forward judge

Generally one bout lasts five minutes, with three minutes allowed for extensions. The time period is measured from the moment a judge has announced *"Hajimé!"* (Begin!). This he does only after the contestants have bowed to each other, touched swords, and crouched in the *sonkyo* position. The match ends with the announcement, *"Shōbu-ari!"* ("We have a winner!")

Point Areas

You gain points by striking your opponent's armor: the *men*, *koté*, and *dō*. Thrusts are permitted to the *tsuki* (throat flap attached to the *men* and surrounding chest area). No other part is considered a point area. Strikes are permitted only to armored parts of the body.

Blows are permitted to the following parts:

Men:

The *shō-men* (which protects the top of the head)
The side parts from the ears and above (*migi-men* and *hidari-men*, also called *yoko-men* <*migi* = right; *hidari* = left; *yoko* = side>)

Dō:

The *migi-dō* and *hidari-dō*.

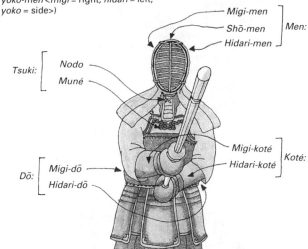

Tsuki: Nodo, Muné

Men: Migi-men, Shō-men, Hidari-men

Koté: Migi-koté, Hidari-koté

Dō: Migi-dō, Hidari-dō

Koté:

The *migi-koté*
The *hidari-koté* (but only when he is holding his sword above his *dō*)

Tsuki:

The throat flap (and the *muné* when he is in the *jōdan-no-kamaé* <sword over head> posture, or when he is armed with two swords)

113

Points for Blows and Thrusts

The judges frequently confer with each other. Points are awarded for well-executed blows and thrusts. A point is given only if all of these three conditions are met: (i) top fighting form; (ii) the blow or thrust is made from a recognized posture with the end third of the *shinai*'s *jimbu;* and (iii) if a blow, it is made accurately on a permitted part of the opponent's body, using the side of the sword opposite the *tsuru*.

In addition, the contestant must exhibit *zanshin* (page 106).

A point may also be given in the following cases:
If, at the moment your opponent drops his sword or falls, you immediately follow up with a valid blow or thrust; or, if your strike succeeds at the same time you fall.

A blow or thrust delivered at the instant one contestant crosses over the line delineating the fencing area might be judged valid, as might strikes made at the moment a signal indicates the end of the bout.

Blows and Thrusts not Recognized

In *aiuchi*, both contestants score a valid point against the other simultaneously. (For example, you hit his *men* and he hits yours, or you hit his *koté* and he hits your *men,* these actions happening at exactly the same time). In such a case no point is awarded.

Foul Play and Penalties

Kendō forbids certain movements and provides for a system of penalties. Basically all rules insist upon two things: show respect to your opponent, and fight fairly. Here are examples of actions not accepted:

(1) Showing disrespect in word or deed to one's opponent, or to the judges. (2 points are awarded to the opponent, and the wrongdoer leaves the floor in disgrace.)

(2) Traversing the demarcation line, with one foot completely outside, or part of the body falling outside, or the sword thrust to the floor outside for support. (For this and the following violations, a warning is given the first time; the second time the opponent is awarded one point.)

(3) A deliberate blow or thrust to any area except a point area (page 113).

(4) Blocking an opponent's footwork, or forcing him outside the fencing area with an unwarranted push or thrust.

(5) Pushing a hand or arm against him unfairly, or clamping his sword between one's arm and side to prevent an attack.

(6) Any action going against the spirit of fairness (such as avoiding combat in an unseemly way, in order to gain time).

Two things are important to become expert in kendō: master the basic movements, and practice respect and politeness from beginning to end.

Polite Salutations

Ritsurei

Look him in the eye, then bend forward about 30 degrees, back straight. Your hands touch your thighs. Remain in that posture for a moment, then, with a feeling of calmness, return to the upright position.

Zarei

In the *seiza* posture (page 82), look at your opponent attentively, then bend forward with composure, back straight. Hands are in front of your knees, facing in at a 45 degree angle. Calmly return to the *seiza* position.

Moving into and out of the *seiza* posture

From a standing position, drop your left knee down first. Stand up with your right leg first. Always keep your back straight, with eyes facing directly forward.

Basic Postures for a Match

When the match begins

(For parts of the sword, refer to page 108.) Hold your *shinai* in the *sagetō* position: sword in your left hand, arm extended down, thumb not touching the *tsuba*, with the *tsuru* (the string running from tip to guard) side down. Next, bring your sword to the *taitō* position: left hand (still holding the sword) touching your waist, thumb on the *tsuba*. Starting with your right foot first, advance three paces. Right hand on the handle goes against the guard, then draws the sword, as from a scabbard. Next the left hand grasps the *tsuka-gashira*. Lower the sword in both hands to the *chūdan-no-kamaé* position (see next page), then crouch.

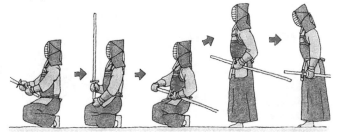

When the match ends

From the *chūdan* position, crouch and return your sword to your left side. Stand up and step back (left foot first) three paces with your sword in the *taitō* position. Return it to the *sagetō* position, then bow.

Kamaé

Kamaé (basic guard positions, with both body and mind alert) are postures you assume when about to attack or repel your opponent. In all of the postures described below, fix your eyes on him as you would on a far away mountain: your gaze penetrates his eyes, but you can perceive his entire body as well.

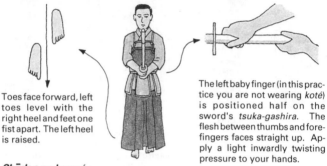

Toes face forward, left toes level with the right heel and feet one fist apart. The left heel is raised.

The left baby finger (in this practice you are not wearing *koté*) is positioned half on the sword's *tsuka-gashira*. The flesh between thumbs and forefingers faces straight up. Apply a light inwardly twisting pressure to your hands.

Chūdan no kamaé

This is the basic posture to prepare for attack. Keep your left hand directly in front of your body, and point your sword towards his throat.

Other *kamaé*

Jōdan no kamaé (sword raised high) is an attack position. *Gedan no kamaé* is defensive, though you can move into an attack by swinging your sword upward to deflect his, if he provides the opportunity. *Hassō no kamaé* does not allow for an immediate attack. *Waki-gamaé* is effective as an attack position, since he finds it hard to judge where the point of your sword is.

Footwork

As explained before, footwork in kendō is second only to vision. Kendō footwork is fascinating. As two examples: when closing in for an attack, the rear foot kicks out powerfully and the right one hits the floor hard; when on guard, feet stay close to the ground, hovering nimbly.

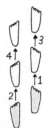   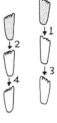

Okuri-ashi

The most basic of all footwork. Thrust out the foot which is closer to the direction you are aiming for, then bring the other foot up close but not past it.

Ayumi-ashi

Similar to ordinary walking, in the sense that one foot passes the other. Used when moving at least 5 paces.

  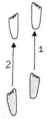

Tsugi-ashi

Used when far from your opponent, but closing in on him. The rear foot comes up close to but remains behind the front one; the front one juts out again. Used only for advancing.

Hiraki-ashi

Use it when dodging and attacking: keep moving, but face him at all times.

Tobikomi-ashi

Excellent for propelling yourself forward to land a blow.

Suburi Sword Exercises

Suburi is a basic exercise, the sword being swung vertically or obliquely. *Suburi* will teach you the feel and action of the sword. It is also used in preparatory and supplementary exercises.

Vertical swing

Start from the *chūdan* posture. Swing the sword straight up above you, then straight down, stopping the tip at knee level. This is good training for hitting the opponent's *men*.

Oblique swing

Starting from the *chūdan* posture, swing the sword up above your head to the right, then down in a line to the left, about 45 degrees from horizontal, then back up to the right, following the same trajectory. When the sword is behind your head again twist it over to your left, then bring it down at about a 45 degree angle to your right.

Practicing Basic Blows and Thrusts

Keep in mind the need to develop your intuition when practicing blows to the *men*, *dō* and *koté*, as well as thrusts to the throat flap. In kendō it is vital that even after you land a blow you remain on guard (*zanshin*), and that you keep facing him.

The ideal space between you and him is *issoku-ittō* (this distance, called *ma-ai*, is often kept in kendō): you can strike him if you move one step forward; one step back and you can dodge his attack.

The sword swoops down as soon as it is raised.

Men-uchi

Start from the *chūdan* position. Swing your sword above you, right hand almost touching your head. Lean forward, darting your right foot forward one step, at the same time swinging your sword down with arms outstretched. Give his *men* a good whack.

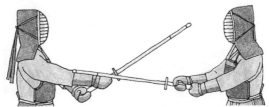

Koté-uchi

Start from the *chūdan* posture. As for *men-uchi*, raise your sword up and dart forward with your right foot. Bring your sword straight down, practically scraping it against his. Bring your left foot up close to the other, and hit him on the right *koté*.

Your fists are directly in front of you at the moment you hit him.

Dō-uchi

Again as in *men-uchi,* swing up your sword from the *chūdan* posture, then bring the tip around and down to your left, simultaneously taking a big step forward with your right foot. Stretch your right arm out straight and whack his *dō* on his right.

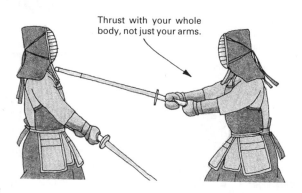

Thrust with your whole body, not just your arms.

Tsuki

This jab at the throat likewise starts from the *chūdan* posture. Stretch out both arms, twisting in your hands at the same time. Dart your right foot forward, thrust out your pelvis, and jab at his *tsuki-daré*.

Uchi-kaeshi

The *uchi-kaeshi* exercise is a repeated cycle of movements. Use a partner to practice footwork and to deliver blows, all the while maintaining the correct distance.

The cycle begins in the *chūdan* posture. Raise your sword well over your head, then bring it down smartly on the top of your partner's *men*. Immediately thereafter hit the sides of his *men*, left right left right in succession, about 5 times. Withdraw the ideal distance, then hit the top of his *men* once again.

KENDŌ TECHNIQUES
応用わざのいろいろ

Once you have mastered the basic blows and thrusts (blows to a partner's *men*, *koté* and *dō*, and thrusts to his *tsuki*), you will have the confidence you need to test your skill against an opponent. Techniques can be divided in two main categories, *Shikaké-waza* (offensive) and *Ōji-waza* (defense plus counterattack).

Shikaké-Waza (Offensive Techniques)

Offensive techniques take advantage of your opponent's being off guard, or else they break down his guard so you can close in for the attack. Here we will discuss *harai-waza* (warding off), *ni-dan* or *san-dan-waza* (two or three steps), *debana-waza* (attacking at the start), *hiki-waza* (stepping back), *katsugi-waza* (shouldering the sword), *katraté-waza* (single hand) and *jōdan-waza* (sword over head).

Harai-Waza (Warding Off)

At the instant your opponent comes at you in an attack, or the moment he has his sword raised somewhat, deflect his sword with an upward swing, then bring it down to deliver a blow.

Harai-dō

You are in the *chūdan* position. Flick your sword to the left below his, then ward it off in a swing to your upper right. This momentum brings your sword above your head, from which position you can swing it down in a circular motion to deliver a blow to his *dō* on his right side.

Ni-Dan or San-Dan-Waza (Two or Three Steps)

This two- or three-step approach is useful when your first blow is unsuccessful but another part of his body is off guard. For example, your sword travels from his *koté* to his *men*, or from *koté* to *dō*. In a three-step action it might move from *koté* to *men* to *dō*.

Koté to men

From the *chūdan* position you raise up your sword and go for his *koté*. He retreats a pace. You immediately take advantage of this by leaping forward one step and hitting his *men*.

Koté to dō

Strike at his *koté* when you are *issoku-ittō* apart. Perhaps he will dodge by raising his hands and retreating one step. This leaves his side open. In a flash you have your sword over your head, to whack it down in a circular motion onto his right *dō*. Next, rush past him. Untense your muscles, face toward him again and maintain *zanshin*.

Debana-Waza (Attacking at the Start)

Grab an opportunity and strike the moment he begins an attack or starts advancing. More than keen observation is needed here: the trick is to intuit his future actions.

Debana-men
You face each other in the *chūdan* position. You sense him moving forward one pace, preparing to strike. If at that moment you see an opening, swing up your sword a little, move forward decisively and deliver a sharp blow on his *men*.

Debana-tsuki
You are both in the *chūdan* position. He budges. The moment you sense this, advance resolutely and jab at his throat flap.

Hiki-Waza (Stepping Back)

Hiki-waza are stepping-back techniques. When you are close to each other, sword guard to sword guard, step back to obtain the ideal distance for a strike. Though not much force is needed here, skill certainly is.

Hiki-men

Your sword guards push against each other. Move back sharply with your left foot, and raise your sword over your head at the same time. This sets him off guard. Bring your sword down on his *men*, then withdraw swiftly.

Hiki-koté

Again your sword guards push against each other. Again you take a big step back with your left foot, at the same time swinging your sword up. Then pull back your right foot and hit his *koté*.

Katsugi-Waza (Shouldering the Sword)

When at a considerable distance from your opponent, suddenly swing your sword up onto your shoulder. This might cause him to defend one part of himself, allowing you to hit another part. Accurate timing may allow you to take advantage of his bewilderment.

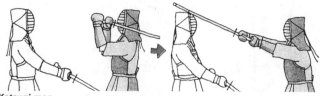

Katsugi-men

When in the *chūdan* position, suddenly pull back your sword and rest it almost horizontal on your left shoulder, at the same time advancing with feet very close to the floor. At the right moment swing your sword from your shoulder, slap down your right foot and hit his *men* with one fell swoop.

Kataté-Waza (Single Hand)

This technique uses only one hand (usually the left one) to thrust at the throat flap, or the left hand to hit the *men*. *Kataté-waza* can be used in attacks from a certain distance, as your arm is outstretched. But a single hand has less power so in many cases the technique will not earn you a point.

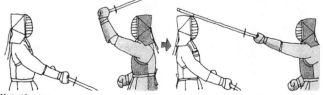

Kataté-men

Stand in the *chūdan* pose, observing his movements carefully. If his sword tip drops back a little, bring yours up over your head, slamming your left foot forward. Your right hand drops from your sword, while your left one, holding it, comes up to ear level. Stretch out your left arm, bringing it down at an angle to hit the *men* on its right side.

Jōdan-Waza (Sword Over Head)

Start from the *jōdan-no-kamaé* posture, with sword over head. The sword is slammed down with tremendous resolve. Most effective if done properly.

Jōdan-men

With sword over your head, grab an opportunity to swing your sword down, at the same time slapping your right foot forward. Your right hand leaves the handle, and your left arm stretches out to hit his *men* hard.

Jōdan-koté

If you see an opportunity when your sword is up and slightly to the left, bring it down in a line parallel to his sword, freeing your right hand. Step left forward, stretch out your left arm and hit his right *koté*.

Ōji-Waza (Defense Plus Counterattack Techniques)

In this second group of kendō techniques your tactics depend upon your opponent's movements, so keen observation is a must. When he comes flying at you, chose the exact moment to move in the required direction (it could be in any direction) and to go on the offensive with the most suitable strategy. Here are four types of ōji-waza:

Nuki-Waza (Dodge then Strike)

In *nuki-waza* you dodge with your body or ward off with your sword, thereby making him slash the air. You are then able to rush in for the kill at the end of his move.

Men-nuki-dō

At the very moment you are certain he is coming at your *men,* dodge his sword by stepping forward with your right foot to oblique right (as if to pass him). Tighten your wrists and swing your sword hard onto his right *dō*.

Koté-nuki-men

His sword is coming at you, aimed at your *koté*. Step back, warding off his blow with your sword, in the same movement nimbly swinging your own sword over your head. At the moment his sword's swing ends in the void, whack his *men.*

Suriagé-Waza (Slide Up the Sword then Strike)

In *harai-waza* you deflect his sword when it is not moving. *Suriagé-waza* is also a warding-off technique, but here you make his sword swerve by sliding yours up along his as he is bringing it down. So in this case not much force is needed.

Koté-suriagé-men

His sword is coming down, aimed at your *koté*. Put out your arms, snap your wrists and slide your sword up at an angle to the right, making his own sword swerve away. Hit his *men* before he has time to blink.

Tsuki-suriagé-men

You see his thrust heading towards your throat flap. When he gets close, slide your sword up along his to make it swerve away. Move forward with your right foot at the same time, and hit his *men* as quickly as possible.

Kaeshi-Waza (Receive, Deflect, then Strike)

You allow him to hit your sword lightly with his, then use the resulting spring action to make his sword bounce back to the other side. This gives you a chance to hit him. You need agility and flexible wrists for this. This *waza* allows you to get at his left or right *men* or *dō*.

Men-kaeshi-migi-dō

Let him get close as he prepares to strike your *men*. Stretch out your arms and receive his sword blow lightly on the left side of yours. His sword is reflected away. Step obliquely right forward (as in *men-nuki-dō*) and strike him hard on the right *dō*.

Dō-kaeshi-men

You see that he plans to strike your *dō*. Let him come close, then move your left foot back half a pace obliquely to the left. The moment his body stretches out, raise your left hand over your head, the sword pointing downward. Receive his sword on yours, then waste no time swinging your sword over your head so as to deliver a good blow on his *men*.

Uchiotoshi-Waza (Hit Down Then Strike)

In this technique you swing your sword down on his, deflecting it. Then you immediately raise your sword up to strike his *men* or *koté*.

Dō-uchiotoshi-men

Observe closely the line his sword makes as it moves towards your *dō*. Swing slightly left back. The instant before he strikes your *dō*, slam your sword down against his sword. Your sword will bounce back: use this force to swing it quickly over your head, then bring it down on his *men*.

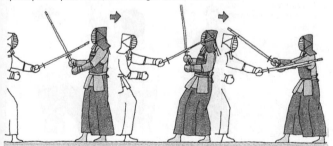

Tsuki-uchiotoshi-men

He is lunging at your throat. Drop back slightly with your left foot, dodging the tip of his sword. At the same time twist your wrists and hit his *men* as soon as his body stretches out its full extent.

Samurai Sword-fighting Movies

Many people like a story where good is pitted against evil, and the Japanese are no exception. Many films are right out of the days of the *samurai,* with plenty of sword-fighting action, called *chambara*.

At the climax we may see the hero at the outlaws' hide-out, gloriously thrusting metal on metal, killing one villain after another until all of the bad guys lie dead.

Engetsu-Sappō: The sword is swung in a circle.

Heroes in such novels and movies have their own special techniques.

Young children, especially boys, used to be fond of make-believe *chambara,* but this kind of rough stuff is dying out.

CHAPTER
5

KARATÉ
空手

Karaté is a unique blend of boxing from China and martial art from Okinawa. In karaté no weapon is allowed, only hands and feet, which must be trained to block, strike and kick. The aim is weapon-less protection, knocking over an aggressor with one blow. But karaté goes beyond achieving physical prowess to include a perfecting of the spirit.

In Japan there are presently more than 50 different karaté styles. These are hard to distinguish properly, but the history of karaté shows us that schools can be divided into three broad categories: (1) Okinawan traditional karaté; (2) a mixture of Japanese *jūjutsu* (page 72) and Okinawan karaté; and (3) a mixture of Japanese *jūjutsu*, Okinawan karaté, and Chinese boxing. The following division of karaté systems might make things clearer:

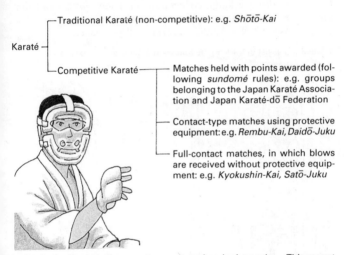

Karaté
- Traditional Karaté (non-competitive): e.g. *Shōtō-Kai*
- Competitive Karaté
  - Matches held with points awarded (following *sundomé* rules): e.g. groups belonging to the Japan Karaté Association and Japan Karaté-dō Federation
  - Contact-type matches using protective equipment: e.g. *Rembu-Kai, Daidō-Juku*
  - Full-contact matches, in which blows are received without protective equipment: e.g. *Kyokushin-Kai, Satō-Juku*

In the beginning karaté was not a sport, and so had no rules. This meant matches as such were not held, for they could have led to injury or even death. But many adherents wanted karaté to be more widely practiced. Karaté therefore grew into a sport with competitive matches governed by definite rules. Most matches are conducted as demonstrations of *kata* forms (a point system is used) or as *kumité* engagement matches. Competition rules vary, generally in accordance with the outline given above.

But competitions are of secondary importance; the essence of karaté lies in basic training, in mastering the *kata* (forms), and in training for *kumité* engagement matches.

137

KARATÉ APPAREL AND EQUIPMENT

服装と用具

Apparel is very similar to that worn in jūdō, though the cloth is thinner since karaté involves no grappling. The *obi* belt is black for those ranked with a *dan,* white for those ranked lower.

As mentioned above, karaté concentrates on defense with no weapon whatsoever. Indeed, rings, necklaces, watches, glasses, etc. must be removed as well. The karaté uniform is all you have.

However, to assist in training the following objects are sometimes used:

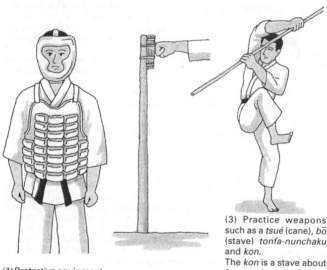

(1) Protective equipment such as a plastic air-cushion face protector and padded vest;

(2) *Makiwara* straw-padded striking post to develop fist technique;

(3) Practice weapons such as a *tsué* (cane), *bō* (stave) *tonfa-nunchaku* and *kon.*
The *kon* is a stave about 2 meters long, tapered at both ends. A number of forms using the *kon* have been taught for ages.

Those wishing to practice karaté will quickly realize the necessity of mastering basic movements and outward decorum, important to karaté as they are to other Japanese martial arts.

Salutations

Next, let your glance descend naturally.

Ritsurei (standing salutation)

Stand to attention with heels together, feet pointing outward at an angle of about 60 degrees. Look him straight in the eye. Bend forward about 30 degrees, back straight. Remain still in this position a moment, then return to your previous standing position.

Your buttocks remain on your heels the whole time.

Zarei (kneeling salutation)

Sit in the *seiza* position (page 82), back straight, eyes facing straight ahead, shoulder muscles not tense. Bow low, placing both hands apart on the floor (left first, right second). Hands rest in front of your knees, with fingers pointing somewhat inward. After a moment return calmly to *seiza*.

Stances

Karaté makes use of a number of stances, all of them basic positions from which you can defend or counter-attack. When moving into the *seiza* posture from a standing position, drop your left knee down first. Stand up with your right leg first.

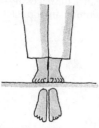

Heisoku-dachi (feet together stance)

Stand to attention, but with toes together. Relax your shoulder muscles.

Musubi-dachi (informal attention stance)

Heels together, toes pointing out about 60 degrees, back straight.

Heikō-dachi (parallel feet stance)

Spread your legs so that your feet, parallel to each other, are apart about the same width as your shoulders.

Hachiji-dachi (natural stance)

Feet apart about the same width as your shoulders, pointing outward about 40 degrees. A very natural position.

Kiba-dachi (horse riding stance)

A basic stance: feet apart about double the length between your shoulders. Feet parallel to each other. Knees bent and pushed apart, as in horseback riding.

Shiko-dachi (squat stance)

Feet apart about 65 centimeters, toes pointing out, trunk lowered and belly jutting out a little.

Fudō-dachi
(immovable stance)

Feet wide apart, one forward, one behind. The back leg is bent out somewhat, the front one bent in a little.

Sanchin-dachi
(hourglass stance)

One foot slightly ahead of the other, front one facing inward about 60 degrees.

Zenkutsu-dachi
(front stance)

One leg placed forward, center of gravity upon it, with the knee bent. Other leg to the rear. Upper body straight.

Kōkutsu-dachi
(back stance)

Place your center of gravity on the leg which you want behind you. Bend the knee, at the same time moving your other leg forward lightly.

Nekoashi-dachi
(cat leg stance)

Starting from the back stance, raise the heel of your front foot. Center of gravity remains on the rear leg.

Body Parts as Weapons

Karaté uses no weapons. That is to say, karaté's weapons are the naked fist, palm, forearm, elbow and foot. So naturally experts keep these parts in good working order.

The Fist

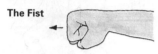

Sei-ken (regular fist)
Clench your fist with the thumb gripping the first two fingers. Punch out so that contact is made on the basal joints of the index and middle fingers and the area below. In *sei-zuki* you punch out with the back of the fist up, while in *taté-zuki* the back faces sideways. In *ura-zuki* the fist back faces down.

Ura-ken (back fist)
Aim your blow so that the basal joints of the index and middle fingers absorb the shock. The back of the fist faces down, and the wrist exhibits a snapping action when hitting.

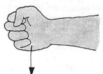

Hira-ken (flat fist)
The four fingers are held together and bent at the first and second joints, basal joints straight, forming a flat surface. The thumb presses against the index finger to lend support.

Tettsui (iron hammer)
A grip similar to the regular fist. Fist back faces out. The arm, bent at the elbow, is thrust out resolutely, the fist hitting like a hammer, the outer side of the fist being the hammer head.

The Palm

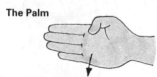

Shutō (sword hand)
The four fingers are held together, straight. The thumb is bent and pressed against the basal joint of the index finger. Hit with the outer side of the hand.

Haitō (ridge hand)
Often contrasted with the sword hand. The thumb is bent, and presses hard against the inside of the index finger, where it must stay.

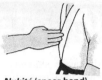

Shōtei (heel of the hand)
From the sword hand position bend the four fingers at the first and second joints. Bend your hand back at the wrist, with palm facing your opponent. Hit with the heel of the hand.

Haishu (back hand)
Your hand is in the sword hand position, but this time use the entire back of the hand. Your forearm swings out from the elbow joint to land a blow.

Nukité (spear hand)
With hand in the sword hand position, stab with your four outstretched fingers.

The Forearm

The forearm (_koté_) is useful for blocking.

The Elbow

Bend the arm far in, then strike with the point of the elbow.

The Foot

Zensokutei or _koshi_ (ball of the foot)
Curl your toes up. Aim your kick so that the ball of the foot absorbs the shock. Useful in _maé-geri_ and _tobi-geri_ (pages 146 & 147).

Kakato (heel)
Push out your heel, pulling the instep towards your lower leg. Kick with your heel.

Sokutō (sword foot)
Pull your instep towards your lower leg, sole facing in. Kick with the outside edge of your foot.

Haisoku (instep)
Curl your toes down towards the soles of your feet, apply pressure at the ankle to straighten your foot out, and kick with the upper surface of the foot.

The Knee

Curl your toes up, then jab with your kneecap. You need very flexible knee and hip joints for this.

BASIC TECHNIQUES
基本技術

All karaté students must first master the basic techniques: *uké* (blocking), *tsuki* (fist thrusts), *uchi* (strikes) and *keri* (kicks).

Uké (Blocking)

Of primary importance is to block your opponent's attack. Blocking techniques can be divided into three: those protecting the upper, middle and lower sections of the body.

Gedan-barai (lower section block)

Move from a ready position into the front stance (page 141), at the same time raising a fist (the one you will use to block) to your shoulder, then swing it down to ward off his attack to the lower half of your body. The fist twists from in to out.

Jōdan-agé-uké (upper section rising block)

When he tries an attack on your head or shoulders, block it with the inside of your forearm.

Chūdan-shutō-uké (middle section sword hand block)

With your hands in the sword hand position, parry any attack to your chest area using a cutting motion.

Tsuki (Fist Thrusts)

In a thrust the fist is a *'yin'* or *'yang'* position.

Basic fist thrust

This can be delivered from a variety of standing positions, such as the natural, horse-riding, and hourglass stances. One fist moves to the side, the other juts straight out. Fists punch in and out alternatively and repeatedly.

Oi-zuki (front punch)

Right front punch: From the front stance, when your left leg is in front, bring your right leg forward, at the same time punching with your right cocked fist which thrusts forward from your side.

***Gyaku-zuki* (reverse punch)**

Right reverse punch: From the front stance, when your right leg is in front, bring your left leg forward, at the same time thrusting your right cocked fist forward from your side.

***Kizami-zuki* (short punch)**

Right short punch: You have finished a right front punch. Push your right foot further forward, pull in your right fist and, practically in the same instant, thrust it out again.

***Kagi-zuki* (hook punch)**

With the back of your fist facing up, and arm bent in the shape of a hook, punch with a horizontal jabbing motion.

Uchi (Strikes)

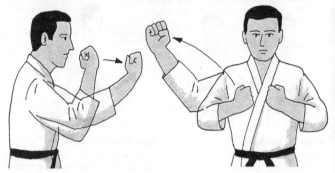

Ura-ken-uchi (back-fist strike)   **Ura-ken-uchi (side strike)**

Keri (Kicks)

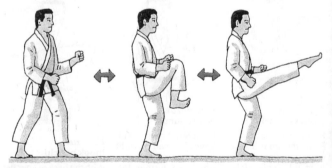

Maé-geri (front kick)

You stand prepared in the front stance. Raise one thigh higher than horizontal, then kick with the ball of your foot. Bring your leg back to its previous stable position.

Mawashi-geri (roundhouse kick)

Starting in the front stance, twist your hips in a circular motion, kicking sideward with your foot, making an arc (your knee is the central point of the arc).

Yoko-geri (side kick)

This is also called the *sokutō-geri* (sword-foot kick). The leg kicks hard with the knee as pivot. As the body swings around to face the opposite direction, the leg kicks up and out with a sword foot (page 143).

Tobi-geri (jump kick)

Leap forward into the air, kicking up and forward with the ball of your foot.

Ushiro-geri (back kick)

Kick upwards and backwards with your heel.

The *Kata*

Kata (forms) practiced in karaté contain a number of defensive and offensive techniques, one flowing into another. The feeling here is that you are up against a number of enemies who are attacking; you must block, thrust with the fist, kick, and even throw. But all movements begin with blocking. After all, in karaté one does not attack first; one defends oneself by blocking, then counterattacks if necessary.

The names of *kata* depend on the karaté style, but here are a few of the important ones:

(1) *Heian* (Peaceful Mind), divided into five forms, from first step to fifth.

(2) *Tekki* (Horse Riding), divided into three forms, from first step to third.

(3) *Bassai* (Penetrating a Fortress)

(4) *Kankū* (Looking at the Sky)

(5) *Gankaku* (Crane on a Rock)

(6) *Jion* (name comes from Jion Temple)

(7) *Enpi* (Flying Swallow)

(8) *Meikyō* (Bright Situation)

CHAPTER
6

OTHER MARTIAL ARTS
その他の武道

Broadly speaking, aikidō sprang from the *daitō aiki* system of early *jūjutsu*. It was one of the practitioners of the *daitō* system, Morihei Ueshiba, who systematized some of the *kata* (established forms used in practice) of *jūjutsu*, and gave the resulting martial art its name, Aikidō. In addition to the style established by Ueshiba there are a number of other aikidō schools as well.

Aikidō's Goals

Aims vary a little, depending on the school, but in every case technique is based on intuition and self-defense: inferring what an opponent has in mind, and rendering ineffective any attack he may try.

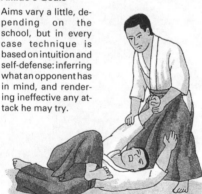

Aikidō Techniques

Hand-to-hand combat can take a number of forms, so aikidō techniques have many variations. Striking, kicking, thrusting and grappling may be done (a) between two people, neither of whom is armed; (b) an unarmed person defending himself against someone with a sword, spear, stave or some other weapon; (c) two armed people; and (d) one person against many. There are also a number of *suwari-waza* (sitting techniques).

In aikidō you must put your technique into effect the moment you make contact—do not give him a chance to counterattack. In a sense all aikidō movements are based on the concept of two people warily facing each other, swords drawn. The stress placed on *metsuké* (fixing one's eyes on his most important point) and *ma-ai* (spacing) call this to mind.

Do not let your upper body tense up. The area of the abdomen is fully alert; it is from here that *'ki'* (physical and psychological power) comes. This energy should be given full play: it rises from your abdomen (which is your core), to exhibit itself in the finger tips of your outstretched hand. The energy so exhibited is referred to as "breath power".

Basic Movements

Aikidō's techniques place importance on two motions, *irimi* and *sabaki*.

Irimi

You face each other. The moment he moves, get out of his line of attack and into his blind side, then stand in the *hammi* posture (feet at right angles to each other, center of gravity slightly forward). For your technique to be effective you must remain on his side.

Move out of the line of his thrust into a blind spot on his side.

Move into his blind spot, out of his stick's line of attack, then knock him over.

Aikidō, as a system of self-defense, attracts many women. Although women are very active in this sport, as they are in other martial arts, this book uses male pronouns throughout, only for ease of expression and simplicity.

Sabaki

Sabaki is controlled body motion. Aikidō movements are often circular, centered around an imaginary point. The body and feet move with fluidity around the center, engulfing and controlling the attacker.

Your fluid motion pulls him into your orbit, allowing you to throw him with a *tenchi-nagé*.

Here the opponent and his stick are considered as one unit. The aggressor, who is holding the end of the stick, can be knocked off balance with it and thrown.

Ukemi

In *ukemi* (receiving a blow) you "roll with the punch", so to speak. Often you are like a spinning top or a ball. *Ukemi* can generally be divided into five types. Three are introduced below; the other two are *yoko-ukemi* (sideways fall) and *maé-chokutō-ukemi* (straight forward fall).

Ushiro hanten ukemi (backward wingover *ukemi*)

Pull back one of your feet, drop a knee to the ground and bring your center of gravity way down. Roll backwards in a circular fashion. When your shoulder hits the ground stop the roll and return to an alert, standing position.

Ushiro kaiten ukemi (backward roll *ukemi*)

Here also you roll backwards, but this time like a ball. After one revolution return to the upright position, ready for the next move.

Maé kaiten ukemi (forward roll *ukemi*)

Roll forward to make one whirl around. Your arms, elbows and shoulders are the rim of a wheel.

Nagé-waza

Aikidō throws (*nagé-waza*) take into account the principles of gravity, momentum and body structure, and are based on circular motion, like a top or a ball.

Shōmen-uchi irimi-nagé

An attacker has his right hand outstretched, ready to chop at you. Jut your right hand out enticingly, so that he hits at it. Pass to his blind side (*irimi*), knock him off balance and drop him.

Kataté-dori shihō-nagé

The *shihō-nagé* (four direction throw) is a typical aikidō *waza*, well illustrating why aikidō body movement is likened to swordsmanship. In this technique you allow him to grab your right wrist with one of his hands. Then you yank it to make him loose balance. His fall follows.

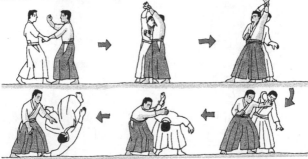

Kataté-dori kaiten-nagé

At the moment he grabs your left wrist with his right hand, swing to your left behind him, pivoting on your left foot. Punch him in the face with your right fist, getting him close to you, his side on your left. With your left hand pull his right hand up and over your head, to bring it down in a slashing motion. Push the back of his neck down to make him roll forward.

Katamé-waza

Katamé-waza (holds and locks) are accomplished by first getting your opponent off balance, then applying a lock to one of his joints. These *waza* can be divided into two types: *omoté*, where you pin him when he is facing you, and *ura*, where you get him facing somewhat away from you to apply a hold.

Moroté-dori udé-osaé (ura)

When your opponent is on your side, gripping your wrist with both of his hands, use your trapped hand as a chopper. Swing in a circular fashion behind him, and pin him with both of your hands at his wrist and elbow joints.

Nagé-katamé-waza

Here you combine a throw (*nagé*) with a lock (*katamé*). Grab his arm and throw him, then lock the same arm and pin him face down. The number of *waza* in this group is limited.

Tsuki-koté-gaeshi

He comes at you to punch you with his right fist. Get into his blind side. Get his fist under control, using your left hand as a chopper. Swing behind him in a circular motion, knocking him off balance. Twist his right forearm to the left to bring him to the ground, then lock his arm.

NAGINATA
なぎなた

The naginata, a kind of halberd, has a long shaft with a curved blade at one end. In the Edo period it was used primarily by women as an art of self-defense, and by *samurai* children who were required to learn naginata techniques. After the beginning of the Meiji period enthusiasts developed naginata wielding into a martial art for women. The blade can be used to cut, slice sideways and to deflect blows. The butt end lends itself to thrusts, strikes and parrying. This versatility means training in the naginata can be put to good effect with other weapons as well, namely the sword, spear and stave.

Weapon and Apparel

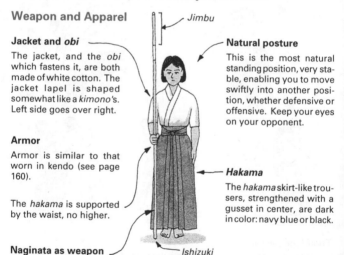

Jimbu

Jacket and *obi*

The jacket, and the *obi* which fastens it, are both made of white cotton. The jacket lapel is shaped somewhat like a *kimono*'s. Left side goes over right.

Armor

Armor is similar to that worn in kendo (see page 160).

The *hakama* is supported by the waist, no higher.

Natural posture

This is the most natural standing position, very stable, enabling you to move swiftly into another position, whether defensive or offensive. Keep your eyes on your opponent.

Hakama

The *hakama* skirt-like trousers, strengthened with a gusset in center, are dark in color: navy blue or black.

Ishizuki

Naginata as weapon

Total length is from 2.1 to 2.25 meters long. The curved blade on one end is made of bamboo, and is 50 cm long. The oak shaft is capped with leather at the butt end.

Standing Alert

In *kamaé* postures you stand alert, ready to defend yourself or to attack. These basic postures are divided into five types, four of which are described below (the fifth is *gedan no kamaé*). Each type can be sub-divided into left and right.

The *kissaki* is a little higher than the *ishizuki*.

The *kissaki* (blade tip) is held at the same height as the adversary's solar plexus.

Chūdan no kamaé

This is actually the basis of all postures, and the best one from which to adapt to your opponent's stratagem or to develop your own. In *hidari* (left) *chūdan*, the left foot is placed forward. The left hand holds the weapon above the right. The body faces the adversary obliquely.

Jōdan no kamaé

From this posture you can attack at will. To assume this position, start from the *chūdan no kamaé*. Change the position of your hands while raising the blade tip, putting your right hand above the left. Thrust the *ishizuki* forward, point the blade up, and stand with the weapon raised high.

Waki-gamaé

You can strike in a flash from this aggressive position. Starting in the *chūdan* posture, raise the *kissaki*, changing the position of your hands. The *ishizuki* swings forward, blade going behind. Hold the naginata horizontal.

Hassō no kamaé

From the *chūdan* posture again raise the *kissaki*, changing hand position, right hand going above. Your right hand goes up to ear level, your left one is at your hip, touching it lightly.

Areas to Aim For

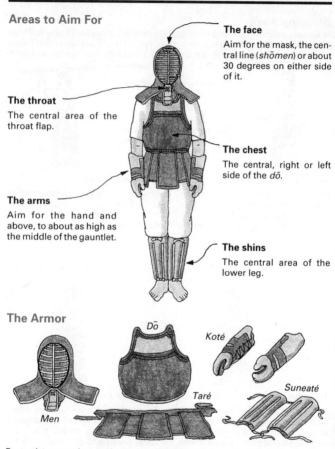

The face

Aim for the mask, the central line (*shōmen*) or about 30 degrees on either side of it.

The throat

The central area of the throat flap.

The chest

The central, right or left side of the *dō*.

The arms

Aim for the hand and above, to about as high as the middle of the gauntlet.

The shins

The central area of the lower leg.

The Armor

Dō

Koté

Suneaté

Taré

Men

Protective armor is worn in naginata matches. The *men*, *dō*, *koté*, and *taré* are very similar to those used in kendō, but shin guards have been added. Equipment is put on in this order: *tare*, *dō*, *suneaté*, *men*, *koté*.

Basic Cuts and Thrusts

The naginata is a flexible instrument. It can be raised high, swung back, thrust out, shifted in position, and so on. This versatility lends the weapon well to cuts and thrusts to the *men*, *dō*, *koté*, and *suneaté*.

Striking the *men* from high

You are in the left *chūdan* position, your right leg to the rear. Bring your right foot forward decisively, swing the naginata over your head, facing her straight on. Take one step forward with your left foot to face her at an angle – swoop the blade down to cut at her mask.

Swinging the naginata around to strike the *men*

Starting in the *chūdan* posture, with the *kissaki* pointing downward, swing the naginata around behind you. At the same time, slide your right hand up beside your left one, face directly forward, and raise the naginata high. Quickly switch hand positions and bring your right foot forward to face her obliquely, moving your left hand to the butt end (right hand in front). Strike her mask.

Thrusts

Chokutotsu: Start in the *chūdan* position. Bring your rear hand to midriff and, in one motion, advance and jab your weapon against her throat flap.

Kurikomi-zuki: Again starting in the *chūdan* position, raise the naginata so that your rear hand is as high as your shoulder. Jut your front foot forward one pace, at the same time turning the blade downward with your rear hand and thrusting at her throat flap.

Receiving blows

Parry blows with the blade or shaft of your weapon.

Receiving a blade cut on the mask (*men-uké*)

Receiving a blade cut on the shin (*suné-uké*)

Receiving a blow from the shaft's central area on the mask

Initiative: Yours or Hers?

Techniques can be divided into two types. In *shikaké-waza* you take the initiative, eliminating her aggressive force or striking after you get her confused. In *ōji-waza* the initiative is first hers: but you render her attack ineffective with your weapon or by moving adroitly out of the way. In so doing you search for an opening, and make good use of it.

<Your initiative> Push her weapon away with your shaft, then thrust with the butt end

Parrying techniques enable you to cut or thrust at any part of her body allowed, after you have warded off her naginata from the front or from behind. One example: move one pace forward from the *chūdan* position, deflect her blade with your shaft, move forward some more and thrust the butt end of your weapon into the side of her *dō*.

<Her initiative> Her attempt on your mask → You eliminate her weapon then thrust

In this technique you block her thrust or cut and, at the same instant, use the curved part of your blade in a twisting motion to make her drop her weapon, allowing you to strike right away. One example: she comes at your mask when you are in the *chūdan* position. Twist her naginata out of her hands with your own weapon. Waste no time in delivering a jab.

KYŪDŌ
弓道

Kyūdō, Japanese archery, has its origins in the distant past, when bows and arrows were used in hunting and on the battlefield. Kyūdō is now a popular sport, but still retains its traditional clothing and polite etiquette. In this way it is the same as other Japanese martial arts and, like them, places emphasis on spiritual training.

Arrows

Arrows are made of bamboo, and are fletched with three bird feathers (which have been cut in mid-length). Arrows are of two types, for targets placed 28 meters away, or for distant targets 60 meters away. Modern arrows may be made of strengthened aluminum.

The Bow

Bows are made of bamboo and wood, or of glass fiber. Three lengths are available, depending on the archer's height: 215, 221, and 227 cm.

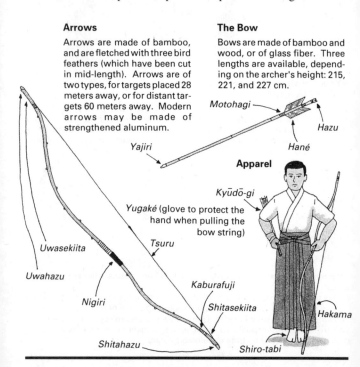

Motohagi

Hazu

Yajiri

Hané

Apparel

Kyūdō-gi

Yugaké (glove to protect the hand when pulling the bow string)

Uwasekiita

Tsuru

Uwahazu

Nigiri

Kaburafuji

Shitasekiita

Hakama

Shitahazu

Shiro-tabi

The Archery Range

As mentioned above, targets are set 28 meters or 60 meters from the archer. Our discussion will be confined to the shorter range.

Mato

A round piece of white cedar wood, 36 cm in diameter and about 10 cm thick, with a paper target stuck on the front.

Kasumi-mato (regular practice)

Hoshi-mato (for official university tournaments)

Sanshoku-mato (for national tournaments): equally spaced concentric circles colored white (outside rim), red and green (center).

Archery ground

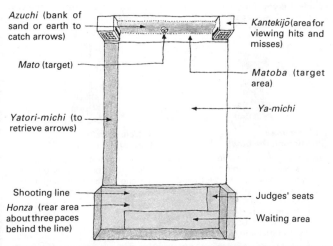

Azuchi (bank of sand or earth to catch arrows)

Mato (target)

Yatori-michi (to retrieve arrows)

Shooting line

Honza (rear area about three paces behind the line)

Kantekijō (area for viewing hits and misses)

Matoba (target area)

Ya-michi

Judges' seats

Waiting area

Shahō-hassetsu

Shooting an arrow involves eight steps, the *shahō-hassetsu*. By skillfully blending these eight steps into a fluid whole your technique will become expert.

Be careful not to sway forward or back. Keep your back straight.

The angle between your legs is about 60 degrees.

(1) *Ashi-bumi* (Positioning the feet)

Stand at the shooting line, your left side toward the target. Align your left foot with an imaginary line coming from the target center, the foot half a pace apart from the other. Look at your feet as you bring your right foot another half-pace apart.

(2) *Dō-zukuri* (Positioning the upper body)

Lean forward a bit, to give the sensation that the gravitational force of your body is flowing through your big toes. Back and neck are straight, shoulders slope down, left hand holds the bow. Fit the arrow to the bowstring and hold it.

(3) *Yu-gamaé* (Positioning the bow)

Place the arrow notch in the bowstring's *nakajikaké*, holding the bow lightly at the *nigiri* with your left hand. Calmly shift your vision from the arrow notch to align it along the arrow to the target, the bridge of your nose splitting the target in two, so to speak. Keep your breathing relaxed.

(4) *Uchi-okoshi* (Raising the arms)

Here concentrate on your right arm. Calmly raise both arms until each is high enough to form an angle of about 45 degrees from vertical.

(5) *Hiki-waké* (Pulling back the arrow)

Push out your left arm, lowering it so that it is horizontal, aligned in the direction your left foot is pointing (the side of your left elbow has come down close to the target line). Bend your right arm, pulling back the arrow horizontally about one third of its length. Tops of both fists remaining horizontal, push the bow forward more with your left hand, drawing back the string at the same time until the gloved hand comes close to your right shoulder.

(6) *Kai* (Positioning the arrow)

The side of the arrow touches your cheek, in line with your lips, practically horizontal. Bow string is next to your side. Tension rests equally between both arms. Hold this position for 5 or 6 seconds.

(7) *Hanaré* (Letting fly)

This is the moment you release the arrow. Arms fly wide apart horizontally. The feeling here is that your chest splits vertically in two.

(8) *Zanshin* (Remaining alert)

Maintain the *hanaré* posture even after you release the arrow, staying alert and aware. Hands remain in the same horizontal line. Eyes rest on where the arrow has hit.

NINJUTSU
忍術

In the age of the warlords the ninja art of subterfuge was most useful in spying, obtaining enemy information, assassinations and under-cover intrigue. Ninja formed a special social class of their own in certain areas of Japan, especially in Iga (present-day Mié Prefecture) and Kōga (Shiga). Ninja techniques were grouped in a number of different styles, including the Iga, Kōga, Takeda, Togakushi and Kusunoki schools.

Tools of the ninja's trade

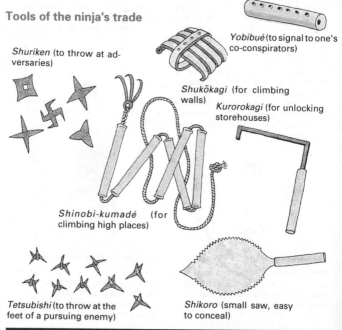

Yobibué (to signal to one's co-conspirators)

Shuriken (to throw at ad-versaries)

Shukōkagi (for climbing walls)

Kurorokagi (for unlocking storehouses)

Shinobi-kumadé (for climbing high places)

Tetsubishi (to throw at the feet of a pursuing enemy)

Shikoro (small saw, easy to conceal)

Ninja strategy adapted to the problem at hand. There were seven different ways to disguise oneself, and all kinds of ways to infiltrate a castle or manor (one way is obvious: befriend a servant working there.) Ninja listed five methods to escape or hide, depending on the subterfuge used: water, fire, wood, earth, or metal.

Suiton no jutsu

In a pond, river or castle moat ninjas hid under the water. To conceal themselves they kept only their faces above water, covered with straw (or whatever) in an obscure area, like under a tree. When completely submerged the ninja could breathe through a bamboo pipe.

Katon no jutsu

Sometimes ninja escaped detection by lighting a fire.

Doton no jutsu

The earth itself provides ample opportunity for invisibility.

Mokuton no jutsu

Ninja were adept at blending in with trees and thickets.

KEMPŌ

いろいろな拳法

Kempō is yet another martial art practiced without a weapon. The hand, either clenched in a fist or open like a chopper, is used in thrusts and blows. The foot is also used. Kempō originated long ago in China, becoming a military technique employed for self-defense. The technique is still widely used there, the aim being to develop a sound mind in a sound body. In Japan a number of kempō styles are practiced, three of which are discussed below.

Taikyokuken

This, another version of Chinese kempō, is representative of the internalized style, where forceful energy is hidden. The body is kept relaxed and pliant. Motion is slow and fluid, keeping time with the rhythm of breathing.

Shōrinji Kempō

One branch of Chinese kempō emphasizes an active, external show of force, with daring, vigorous attacks. *Shōrinji kempō*, which originated about 1500 years ago, is a typical example of this style. But as practiced today the school draws on techniques introduced into Japan in 1947 by So Do-shin. This school does not determine winners and losers in combat. Rather, emphasis is placed on training and on exercises between two people, each taking turns in applying basic techniques on the other.

Nihon Kempō

In 1932 the ancient Japanese *jūjutsu atemi-waza* (knockdown blows and thrusts using the fist, elbow, and other body points) were reintroduced as hand-to-hand combat. At the time it was called *Dai-Nippon Kempō*. A number of blows, thrusts and kicks can be delivered with the fist, open hand as chopper, elbow, sole or side of the foot, or instep. During practices and matches protective equipment is used.

CHAPTER 7

MODERN-DAY SPORTS IN JAPAN

日本でさかんなスポーツ

Baseball

Baseball and sumō vie for first place in popularity in Japan. Games are broadcast live every day throughout the country during the professional baseball season. Amateur baseball clubs are found in most schools and universities, and workers get into the act as well.

Professional baseball players are divided into two leagues, Central and Pacific, each supported by six corporations owning the teams. 130 games are played annually (these are the "Pennant Races"), with the best teams competing in the Japan Series.

Sports tabloids give a detailed report of the previous day's game, with plenty of interviews with coaches and players. These pages are avidly read by workers at every echelon.

The eyes of the entire nation are on senior high school students competing at national baseball tournaments held twice a year (spring and summer) at the Kōshien Stadium. It is common for losing teams to take a bit of sand from the stadium back to their schools, as a memento.

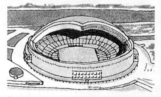

Rain is no problem at the two domed stadiums in Japan, located in Tokyo and Fukuoka. These stadiums can be used for concerts and other events as well.

Soccer

With the advent of Japan's professional soccer league (J. League) in 1993, Japan now has another professional sport, in addition to others such as baseball, sumō and golf. Previously, matches were organized in the Japan League with ten teams supported by companies, with two round robins. The J. League has ten clubs, each representing a Japanese city or town. Each club will compete in 36 games a year, half of them on their own home turf.

Each J. League club is allowed three foreign players, and most teams have wasted no time in hiring soccer stars from areas of the world where soccer is king (like Europe and South America).

Club fans hold up large banners, blow whistles, and generally go bonkers. Quite a few paint their faces in the colors of the team they support.

Local leagues also enjoy support in many cities, and the game is growing in popularity among young people.

Relay Races and Marathons

Japan has many long distance runners, and world-class athletes are invited to the many international marathons held here.

Japan has developed its own form of relay race, the *eki-den,* a long-distance race on ordinary roads. Each contestant runs from 5 to 20 km, with the entire course broken up into more than ten segments. The university relay race from Tokyo to Hakoné and back (held every year on January 2 and 3) is well known.

Marathon runners and relay racers find the roads lined with supporters who urge them on with small paper banners.

Marathons held in New York and Hawaii are seeing more and more amateur Japanese participants every year.

Golf

It is only fairly recently that young men and women have become interested in golf. Women, especially young women, are now often seen at golf schools, and colorful golf wear has become fashionable.

But joining a golf club, or even playing the game, is far from cheap in Japan. So in many cases it still remains the domain of middle-aged men who are comfortably well-off. And of course the game lends itself to companies who wish to entertain important guests.

Golf driving ranges are called *uchippanashi*, or 'nonstop swings'. Most ranges are surrounded by a huge, high net to catch balls, and have at least two floors for driving.

Many amateurs are taking up golf, so courses are crowded and long waits and slow playing can make people irritable. With this drift away from exclusivity, some players complain about a lack of politeness.

In recent years many professional golf tournaments are being held in Japan, attracting the best golfers Japan and the world at large can offer. Games have many spectators, and are broadcast on television.

Skiing

Young people flock to skiing for a good time, and the sport is becoming more competitive as well. Recently Japanese skiers are making their names in the World Cup, Winter Olympics, and other international competitions.

Plenty of money goes into ski wear, as design and fashion change each year.

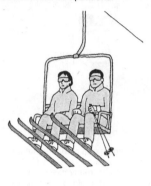

Ski slopes can get very crowded. Patience may be needed when you are waiting for the ski lift.

Many downhill skiers, especially those who belong to university clubs, get involved in other skiing activities, like free style and snow boarding.

Indoor ski slopes using artificially slippery slopes are becoming available for enthusiasts who can't wait for winter.

Tennis

In the 1980s tennis enjoyed a boom among the young crowd. It was fashionable then to walk in the city flaunting a racket. These boom days have died down, but tennis has been adopted by many people, especially those in their twenties, but not only them. One can now see families, including grandparents and grandchildren, playing together.

Beach Volleyball

Tug of War

Volleyball played on sandy beaches in Japan has almost the same rules, but of course bare feet and swim wear are de rigueur. This game has been imported from the U.S., and is now developing its own professional players.

Tug of war became a kind of ceremony in 16th century Japan, the result being used by fortune-tellers to predict the yield from fields or the catch from the sea. The sport is now widely seen at school sports meets, and is even spreading to universities and grown-ups, with national tournaments.

Fishing

Fishing has always been popular, but the number of enthusiasts is now growing even more, perhaps because of the current zest for nature. Japanese people eat a lot of fish, so many enjoy waiting patiently in valley streams or on the coast for that bite which will ensure a fresh meal.

Salt water fishing

Salt water fish can be caught by casting a line from the shore. But many fishermen would rather go out to sea a little to try their luck.

Funayado

The real enthusiast will stay overnight in the home of a boat owner, then set out early in the morning. Sometimes the owner will cook the catch for his guests.

Fishing upstream

For some people, nothing is better than standing by (or in) a mountain stream, fishing for *yamamé* (trout) or *iwana* (char).

Gyotaku

When you catch a big one it is a custom to make a fish print to keep as a memento (or proof?). Chinese ink is rubbed on the fish so that a print can be made. Some people even frame the rubbing.

Camping

Camping, especially the relaxed variety using cars, has been quite popular for the entire family since the mid 1970s. Some throw the tent in the car and set off for the wilds, but others invest more money, converting minivans into mountain cabins on wheels. Many camp grounds are equipped with showers, toilets, maybe even a hot spring.

Hiking and Mountain Climbing

Canoeing

With nature and the environment more in the public eye now, hiking and mountain climbing have become very popular. City folk take off for nearby mountains and streams to enjoy hiking and maybe even camping.

Here again the love for nature comes into play. Kayaks and Canadian-style canoes are both popular. Don't forget a life jacket and, for white-water kayaking, a helmet. The greater your skill, the more you can enjoy rivers and coastal waters.

Marine Sports

Young people since the 1970s have taken to the ocean, which is ideal for an active time, especially surfing. Scuba diving is now very popular as well.

Surfing

Surfing came to Japan in about 1960, and about 10 years later it started to experience a real boom among the young crowd. The boom has since leveled off, but at a high level, with professional surfers now appearing on the scene.

Board Sailing

Board Sailing races and contests are now held regularly at Japan's beaches.

Personal Water Craft

This cross between a motor cycle and a surf board is also sold under the name "Jet Ski" or "marine jet." This is a new water sport, rapidly gaining in popularity. Enthusiasts hold noisy races and competitions.

Scuba diving

Scuba divers have the chance to observe and photograph underwater life, and to explore drowned caves. Many Japanese now spend time in diving schools, hoping to get a license. And the number going overseas specifically to scuba dive is increasing yearly.

Athletic Clubs

These clubs, boasting the best in fitness equipment and swimming pools, are for members only. A growing number of housewives and young women are joining them. To belong to the best clubs has become a status symbol.

First your condition, height, and weight are measured, to determine what program is best for you.

Most clubs have the latest equipment to match your own physical condition, and can measure your blood pressure and pulse when you want.

Pools are open throughout the year. Many people use only the pool. Clubs are now seeing maternity swimming courses and pool programs to get rid of back aches and pains.

Some clubs also have special aerobics studios, always popular with women, married or single, young or old.

GAMBLING AT THE RACES

ギャンブル性のあるスポーツ

Horse Races

Placing money on horses has been around a long time, but because of efforts being made by the Japanese horse racing association, and because of the appeal of young jockeys, the number of racing fans has increased over the last few years, especially among young women. The atmosphere has changed from simply trying to win money to having a good time at the races.

The Japanese horse racing association manages 10 major tracks throughout the country, operating mainly on the weekend. There are a number of highly popular GI races, the most prestigious of which are the Emperor's Prize, Satsuki Prize, Japan Derby, Oaks, Kikka Prize, Arima Memorial Prize, and the Japan Cup.

Before you put money on a horse, consult one of the tabloids dedicated to racing. Some people even get advice from race experts who can (?) predict the outcome.

Nowadays we see many young women lined up to buy pari-mutuel tickets.

Fans always flock to a winning horse, and stuffed dolls of favorites sell well.

Women fall for handsome young jockeys, especially if they win often. Jockeys may be placed on the same level as media stars. The track has a growing number of female jockeys too.

Bicycle Races

You can put your money on professional bicycle racers, just as you would on a horse. Bike races, increasingly popular among young people, are run primarily by local authorities at about 50 tracks throughout Japan.

The race track, paved with asphalt or concrete, is pitched steeply at the curves for easy turns. Races are between many cyclists, and are usually 1 km or more.

Bicycle wheel diameter is 27 inches. Before qualifying, cyclists must train for one year at a special school.

Prize money depends on race track profits. Some champions have been known to earn more than 100 million yen in one year.

Boat Races

Betting is also done on professional speedboat drivers. Amateur boat races were held before World War II, but in the post-war period the need to raise money prompted local government authorities to sponsor professional racing.

Two points in the water are marked out, 300 meters apart. Boats race three times around, making a total of 1800 meters. Suspense is high until the end, as the first boat to make it to one point may not necessarily get around the corner first.

Speedboats are made of wood (3 meters long, 130 cm wide, weighing 70 kg). Basically there are two shapes, the hydroplane type, a flat bottom with two protrusions, and the runabout type, with an evenly-shaped hull. The outboard motor, made in Japan, can get up to about 80 km/h.

Recently the racing world is seeing female racers too going home with large sums of prize money.

INDEX

英文 日本絵とき事典 16

ILLUSTRATED
MARTIAL ARTS & SPORTS IN JAPAN

初 版 印 刷　1993年8月15日
初 版 発 行　1993年9月1日
　　　　　　（Sep. 1, 1993 1st edition）
編 集 人　神部隆志
発 行 人　岩田光正
発 行 所　JTB 日本交通公社出版事業局
　　　　　〒150 東京都渋谷区道玄坂1-10-8 渋谷野村ビル7階
印 刷 所　交通印刷株式会社

●スタッフ
企画・編集　JTB出版事業局 編集二部
　　　　　　外語図書編集 担当編集長　黒澤明夫
　　　　　　編集部直通　☎03-3477-9566
取材・編集協力　株式会社アーバン・トランスレーション
イラスト　松下正己
表紙デザイン　東 芳純
翻　　訳　Nathan Mathews, Urban Connections.

●JTB発行図書のご注文は
JTB出版販売センター
〒150 東京都渋谷区道玄坂1-10-8 渋谷野村ビル7階　☎03-3477-9588

●広告のお問合せは
JTB出版事業局広告部　☎03-3477-9531

934297　712161
ISBN4-533-01995-1